uncommon
WEALTH

You are your best asset – Invest in yourself!

uncommon
WEALTH

You are your best asset – Invest in yourself!

Phillip Ramsey & Bryan Dewhurst

www.BookpressPublishing.com

Published in Des Moines, Iowa, by:

BookPress Publishing
P.O. Box 71532, Des Moines, IA 50325
www.BookPressPublishing.com

Publisher's Cataloging-in-Publication Data

Names: Ramsey, Phillip, author. | Dewhurst, Bryan, author.
Title: Uncommon wealth : you are your best asset - invest in yourself! / Phillip Ramsey & Bryan Dewhurst.
Description: Des Moines, IA: BookPress Publishing, 2021.
Identifiers: LCCN: 2020923368 | ISBN: 978-1-947305-25-0
Subjects: LCSH Finance, Personal. | Success. | Success in business.| Investments. | Debt. | Self-actualization (Psychology) | Conduct of life. | BISAC BUSINESS & ECONOMICS / Personal Finance / Money Management | SELF-HELP / Personal Growth / Success
Classification: LCC HG179 .R31575 2021 | DDC 332.024/01--dc23

First Edition

Printed in the United States of America
10 9 8 7 6 5 4 3 2 1

We would like to dedicate this book:

To everyone who has felt there was a better way to build wealth than through traditional means.

To our families who have been so supportive throughout our lives. You are constantly supporting, encouraging, and sacrificing for us so we can do what we do best. Thank you.

To our amazing clients and friends for sharing their lives with us. This book is the common denominator and intersection of all your stories as you pursue the Uncommon path. Thank you for trusting us and letting us co-pilot your amazing journey!

To Craig Landes, Words Beyond Content, and Bookpress Publishing for helping us present our thoughts and ideas in this book.

Lastly, we want to thank God as He has gifted to us a platform to encourage others to use their unique gifts to create amazing things and impact others.

CONTENTS

.

Introduction

This is not a book to tell you how awesome we are. A book like that would be a waste of time. You don't generally care about our goals; you care about yours.

You are the hero of this story, not us. This is the secret to unlocking your true Uncommon Potential.

What follows is a four-part framework that will change the way you look at building a financial foundation. Then we walk through the seven high-level ways to invest and generate residual income.

Each year, we help hundreds of businesses and families to stop sending their money to everyone else and clarify their goals to start investing in themselves. This guide will work for you, regardless of your profession or starting position, because these are principles you can build from.

To get the most out of this book, we encourage you to do three things:

1. Read the book and understand our four-step process

2. Read the book and understand the seven sources of residual income

3. Clarify and complete your goals and the Uncommon
   Financial Dashboard.

Building wealth has changed. Businesses and families that clarify their message, invest in things they can control, and double down on what makes them uncommon find this method is the more fulfilling way to build Uncommon Wealth.

May we all be richly rewarded for putting our goals and values ahead of blindly investing in things we don't truly understand.

CHAPTER 1

Welcome to the Red Pill of Finance

It was our first meeting with Keesia and Shawn. They were like many of our clients—in their 40s, married with children, halfway through their working years, feeling trapped in their careers and skeptical of financial advisors. They were reluctant to meet but had heard from some people that we weren't like the other guys, so they showed up and were ready to talk.

They talked. We listened. We asked questions. They answered. We encouraged them as they started to rethink their plans and dream again!

We are all in the same position as Keesia and Shawn. We have amazing gifts, but most of us need someone to help us unlock our talents. All they needed was a plan created for their risk tolerance to enable them to do it.

Up to this point, Keesia was working at a marketing firm and struggling to go to work every day. Shawn was working in a family business and did not feel challenged. But when we started talking about the opportunities ahead, we noticed a change in their demeanor. The skepticism disappeared. They started sharing what they were passionate about and what they really wanted to do. They started getting excited about the possibilities. And we hadn't even talked about money yet.

At the end of our meeting, we realized Keesia needed to start down a new path. She needed to create her own marketing firm. To do that, she needed a business plan, business name, targeted clientele, and a client acquisition plan. Meanwhile, we tasked Shawn with getting a handle on their spending and monthly expenses. We asked them to track their expenses for the next three months.

The next time we met, they knew what their monthly expenses were. Keesia had picked out a business name, mapped out a business plan, and identified her clientele. They did so much work in two months. Their enthusiasm about changing their lives was contagious. But halfway through the meeting, Keesia called a time-out. All the work she'd done had made her realize something: she didn't want to start a marketing firm. She had figured out what she was passionate about and what she wanted to spend the rest of her life doing. She told us a story about her mother-in-law asking Keesia to write her obituary. She explained how honored she felt writing the final story of someone's life and how she'd written obituaries for many loved ones. She realized she was an obituary expert. More importantly, she knew she wanted to help people write good obituaries and legacy stories for their family members. By the end of her story, we all had tears in our eyes and knew she'd made an amazing decision. "So that's my idea. Is it crazy?" she asked.

"No!" we erupted. "It's not crazy. It sounds incredible! How can we help?"

From then on, our meetings with Keesia and Shawn have been planning sessions to help them maximize their finances, streamline their budget, and empower Keesia to help as many people as she can creating digital products to help the masses. We are thrilled to report that she's dominating at her new business and helping more and more people every day.

You can hear more about Keesia's entrepreneurial story on our podcast, **https://www.uncommonwealth.com/podcasts/keesia-wirt**.

The final part of this story is a shout-out to Shawn, the spouse who believed in and supported his partner's dream. It's not easy stepping back and allowing your spouse to pursue her dreams. But that's what he did. And we have seen time and again how influential a supportive spouse is to the success of the endeavor. Now that Keesia is on a new path, we're so excited to help Shawn unlock his unique gifts and share them with the world. It is time for Shawn to start his Uncommon Path, and Keesia will be beside him to help achieve his Uncommon Wealth.

Welcome to the Path of Uncommon Wealth

Uncommon Wealth is the pursuit of monetizing your passion within a holistic financial plan. Uncommon Wealth will help you design the life you want to live right now while utilizing and building passive streams of income to provide for the future. Wealth transcends finances and encompasses your whole self, good and bad experiences, core values, and your give-back to society. Are your relationships, hobbies, spiritual, social, and physical well-being self-aligned and taken into account by your financial plan? Are you designing a life you are excited to live?

When it comes to planning for your present and future, there is a better way.

So many people dream of retirement, because that's when you do what you really want, instead of someone else telling you what to do.

What if you could do what you love every day? When would

you want to stop doing that? The answer is, "Never!"

Instead of just dreaming about retirement, what if you could stop dreaming and do what you want to do starting right now?

That is what we call Uncommon Wealth.

Let's start redefining retirement.

We have been on this path for nearly a decade, both individually and together as a business. We are excited to share what we have learned with you.

Why We Wrote This Book

As we work with clients, it's amazing what we discover together. Building wealth is about more than the standard set of investment products you've been told are the path to retirement and financial freedom.

We wrote this book from our personal experience and through the process of helping clients find their uniquely Uncommon Path.

Too often, financial planners make you feel guilty for not saving enough today so you can retire in 20 or 30 years. But what's worse is looking back with regret on a path not taken. Finding a financial way forward based on what you are passionate about and good at is the heart of the uncommon path to time freedom.

Traditional financial planning can stifle people's passions and interests in the name of saving for the last day of your life. How sad is that? Our philosophy is the exact opposite. We want to help you keep more money in your pocket now *and* think about the present and the future you want for yourself and your family. As you do, you will have more wealth and understanding of how to achieve time freedom faster and more sustainably.

Building wealth should be about more than saving for your distant future. Every single client we meet with has a story. They have something beautiful they want to accomplish. Often the goals we uncover together are for one to three years out, yet most financial planning is based on the idea of hiding money away for 20 to 30 years. Why? Because financial institutions and advisors are incentivized to take and invest your money for the long-term. Financial institutions profit from having your money for a long time. They want it consistently and to give you back as little as possible. A good example of this is your 401(k) withholding that is taken out of your paycheck every pay period.

We believe another way is possible. We believe there is something beautiful inside you. You have dreams, goals, and ideas that shouldn't have to wait for retirement. Because here's the thing we've learned: when you invest strategically in the way you were made, the way you are gifted, and what fires you up, you can actually make more money, have more joy, and live a life that you desire.

For many, the real problem isn't dreaming or having ideas, it's investing in yourself and organizing those ideas and your money to support your dreams. Traditional financial planning doesn't support those ideas because the way the industry is set up, it can't make money from them.

We want to give you tools throughout this book to help you down this path. More than anything, we want to help you unlock what is beautiful inside you. And we want to help you love your life and how you give back to the world right now.

Those dreams—and that drumbeat inside you that won't let those dreams die—are why we wrote this book.

The Uncommon Wealth Path is a lot like parenting. It's hard. Sometimes you will feel like you are making a mistake. It's unpredictable, but as time passes and you stick to your guns and principles, you see a richer and deeper path. Soon it will be hard to imagine life any other way. Just like raising kids brings a lot of unexpected challenges, but mostly overwhelming joy, so does the Uncommon Path. That is why we *had* to write this book.

The Middle Ground between Dave Ramsey, Tony Robbins, and Robert Kiyosaki

This book is meant to be a guide for anyone wanting to build an Uncommon Wealth Path. For some context, here is a framework to understand where we are coming from in our approach to helping people plan for the immediate and distant future.

Obviously, we have learned a great deal from many people. There are a number of "gurus" people turn to when it comes to breaking through to financial and personal freedom. Three that come to mind are Dave Ramsey, Robert Kiyosaki, and Tony Robbins.

We get a lot of inspiration from them, but we also see how our approach fills in some gaps these men seem to leave. This book and our approach is a way of bridging those gaps.

Here's what we mean: Dave Ramsey (no relation to Phillip) is really great at honing in on budgeting and paying down debt. That's great. Living above your means is not a viable path for anyone in the long term. A budget is certainly like the front lines of a war. If you lose the front line, you are probably going to lose the war. Like Omaha Beach and our stand on D-Day, it was all about winning the front lines in Europe, to give us a foot hold, so the rest of our troops could move in. Dave Ramsey hates debt of all kinds and rails against its use or purpose. We would agree in relation to consumer-related debt, but there are ways of leveraging debt to your advantage when it is backed by an asset or business. We like to help people explore those possibilities if it makes sense for their plan and risk tolerance. Getting rid of debt might not always be the first step into this Uncommon Path.

Robert Kiyosaki's book, *Cashflow Quadrant*, is one of our absolute must-read books for financial mastery. Kiyosaki does a great job of casting vision, but he's a little bit light on how to get there. His Rich Dad/Poor Dad empire is all about finding sources of residual income. We are huge fans of residual income but want to help people find their own specifically customized path into those sources with tangible action steps. A myth of residual income is that it's a one-time effort or push, and then the money will just roll in. That couldn't be further from the truth. Residual income is hard. It takes patience, capital, and discipline, but it's worth it in the end.

Tony Robbins is inspirational and motivational. He does an excellent job inspiring people and helps you pull out what's inside of you and/or what's blocking you from achieving your goals. He creates an environment for you to look inward and be honest with yourself. But beyond inspiration is the hard work you have to do to be successful in any endeavor.

We will bring all of that together and more in Uncommon Wealth.

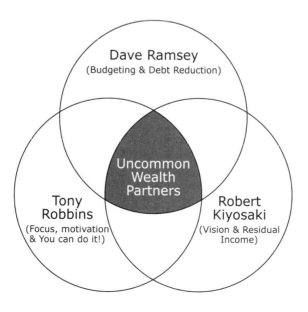

In *Uncommon Wealth: You are your best asset – Invest in yourself*, we want to provide a path for you to embrace the Uncommon Mindset, to walk you through a process that will ultimately lead you to time freedom, and to share examples of those succeeding in going before you in pursuit of Uncommon Wealth.

Let's begin your journey to fully realizing the Uncommon Life!

CHAPTER 2

The Problem with Building Wealth Today

There are plenty of established financial planning organizations out there, so why didn't we just join the crowd in one of those companies? It's simple. We saw firsthand how broken the current financial system can be. We were a part of it, and for us it was just not a good fit. We set out to create a different way.

At the end of the day, financial planning is about income. That is the endgame. The goal is financial freedom. Traditional financial planning is all about investing through the stock market, mutual funds, index funds, bonds, and annuities to provide that lifetime income in retirement.

But there are so many ways to produce income outside just investing in the stock market. That's why we are so passionate, why we love to work with clients, and why we wanted to share our ideas for financial freedom with you.

Don't get us wrong, investments in the stock market are not a bad thing. Every day we help clients with investments, with evaluating social security income, pension income, and investments to produce income. It's just that there is so much potential for building wealth beyond these sources. Too often that potential goes untapped.

Many of our clients come to us saying things like:

"I don't need any more of those kinds of investments."

"My parents' path of working one job and retiring at 65 worked for them, but that's not what I want."

"How do I retire sooner?"

"What can I do before age 59-and-a-half for income when the government tells me I cannot access those retirement plan funds?"

"How do I retire without relying on social security because I am not sure it will be there?"

"I have a great idea for a business. How do I start it, quit my job, and not go bankrupt?"

We started a podcast called, "The Uncommon Life Project." We did this in part to highlight what we call the Seven Sources of Residual Income, which we will be digging into in later chapters. Through the podcast, we share stories of awesome people who are designing the life they want today by doing things that produce income now, not after they retire. We interview people who are building a bridge to the life they feel called to, and we find out how they did it.

This book is our way of sharing these principles at a high level so you can begin to imagine how to take your dreams and turn them into a plan for the present and future.

Here is an example to make this point crystal clear. Recently, we were meeting with another advisor who runs a successful retirement income practice. We respect him a lot. After talking for a while, he shared that he was investing in a brewery. It's an interest of his, and he thought the return potential was really strong. He's also part of a group starting a bottling company to bottle the beer, and opening a bar, so that they have distribution built in and aren't subject to distributors and have one more avenue for selling their product.

We looked at each other and smiled. He is Uncommon. This is

exactly what we are about. We help people tap into their passions to create sources of income for now and the future. We liken it to a drumbeat inside that you just can't ignore.

The problem is that our industry is only really set up to get paid on trapping your money into investment products over long periods of time because those are the products that financial advisors are compensated for.

Why do we see this as a problem? This path of financial planning sets your wealth as a long-term goal that you can't access today, so you just forget about it for now. Most often it ties up your money where you can't touch it, and the advisor has little incentive to help you beyond that.

You'll get that money someday, but until then, stay on that hamster wheel and keep running.

Too often, there is a disconnect that leaves people feeling trapped and worried, hoping that the scenario they laid out turns into reality. Will the 401(k) provide the return as promised? Who knows? It seems that none of our clients have as much as they thought they would in their 401(k) at retirement.

The Millionaire Next Door

Did you know the average millionaire has six to seven streams of income? That does not mean six or seven investment accounts all invested in the same thing. More than likely, it means they have investment income, rental income, social security income, royalty income, and/or business income. In other words, they are truly diversified.

Being able to achieve income from some of these sources is actually a lot easier than people think. It creates consistent income and helps you build wealth now in more dynamic ways. Phillip often says that our clients are really smart people, and when they are educated on all of their options and presented with ideas on other ways to generate income, people will inherently make the best decision for themselves.

Like the millionaire next door, you can have your money do multiple things for you at the same time. Take the example of owning real estate. Someone will pay you rent for the use of that property right now. If you purchased the property through a mortgage, you are leveraging the bank's money. You have cash flow because the renter is likely paying the cost of mortgage, taxes, insurance, and hopefully a bit more on top of all that. Over time, you can raise rent because of inflation. The home or building should appreciate over time. So right there your money is working three different ways to build you wealth.

Real estate is just one example. We wanted to help people not only understand these sources of residual income, but help them build customized strategies that consider their unique situation and goals.

In our experience, traditional financial planning is just not doing this.

The Breaking Point

What if financial planning helped you beyond traditional investments? What if there was something beyond the "set it and forget it" plans that make up most of the marketplace in financial planning?

We wanted to find out.

For Bryan, the breaking point came after years of seeing a couple of things: the power of owning a business, and the powerlessness of being dependent on the ups and downs of a retirement instrument.

When he went into consulting and got to work with companies

like Union Pacific, Berkshire Hathaway, MidAmerican Energy, and GEICO Insurance—some of the most storied names in business— he looked under the hood. He saw that these companies literally made money every second and had so many ways to be paid. The power of cash flow from a view few people have the opportunity to experience left a big impression.

Yes, he studied stocks and how to value them while in college, and talked about that a lot at his mom's brokerage firm. But it was extremely profound to actually see it week in and week out working with these companies from the inside before numbers were consolidated. It was incredible to meet the people responsible and see that the systems that ensure revenue and expenses are recorded correctly. He saw from the inside out how the machine was built to generate hundreds of millions and even billions of dollars.

Phillip was working for a financial services company and was just not feeling inspired by the work. Thinking back on that time, he remembers, "They recruited me because I was breathing and had family and friends."

It was all about hitting up his sphere of influence to set up meetings about their financial future. Family and friends were happy to talk, but it got weird and awkward pretty quickly. He had a pitch to give them, a set of products to sell, and the details of their situation didn't matter too much.

That approach is not Phillip at all. It was a job, and he needed the money, but it couldn't last. Here is how he describes the very last straw:

> What was broken about this approach came into laser-focus for me when I invited my sister and her husband over for dinner so I could tell them all about my new job and what I could do for them.
>
> I was so psyched to tell them about what I was doing and

*then get their money. We were having a nice dinner conversa-
tion and catching up after not seeing them for a while. My wife
and our guests were deep in conversation, and I was not
listening. I was only thinking about when I could tell them how
many ways I could help them with their money.*

*But about halfway through the meal, I got really
conflicted. This was my sister. This was my family. I didn't want
to sell them. I just needed to listen and stop making it about me
and my agenda. From that moment on, I realized it wasn't
about me and my agenda at all; it should be about being
present and truly listening. Who cares about their money? If
they have a need or a question, they will ask. This was the key
to how I wanted to build my career.*

It's Time for a New Toolbox

While traditional financial planning is focused on "Later
Money," we decided to focus on how to leverage "Now Money" to
fuel people's passions today *and* in the future.

For that task, the old toolbox of financial planning simply does
not do the job.

After living these experiences, we were both ready to try
something new. Something had to give. Both of us were miserable,
but Bryan had an idea.

We met over coffee, thinking we were going to commiserate
about our experiences. We quickly realized we were not only in a
similar place, but we both valued the same things. We both wanted
to turn this industry on its head. We each brought a completely
different skill set to the table that complemented each other. When
Bryan turned to Phillip and said, "I know a different way. I just don't
know how to simplify it for others," that is what started this journey.

Phillip was skilled with people and building phenomenal relationships. He didn't want to ruin those relationships just selling products and trapping people's money. Bryan had been living and breathing every aspect of the financial world since he was a kid. Both of us truly wanted to help people to change their concept of what was possible today, not 20 to 30 years from now.

So that's how we started.

We are providing people with new tools for building wealth and a life that is satisfying and aligned with the gifts, talents, and dreams they have been given.

We have been seeing the power of helping people reclaim their dreams, start fulfilling them now, and build wealth. We help people save for the long-term while encouraging them to build on and leverage what they have right now.

It is absolutely amazing.

The Myth of Diversification

The general problem we are solving is the idea of hiding your money away in instruments you can't touch until a magical age of retirement. It's time to look at some of the specific challenges we see in this approach. It starts with the myth of diversification.

To be clear, we are not opposed to diversification. You don't want all your financial eggs in one basket. But again, there is a problem with how financial planning is practiced. The myth of diversification is that putting your money in different accounts or different mutual funds with asset allocation is diversification. It's not.

Too often with this approach, you are putting money into instruments that all basically do the same things. An IRA and 401(k) tie up your money until you are almost 60, and they invest your money in similar ways to grow your money over time.

We are here to tell you that having a few retirement accounts is not diversification. That is using one tool, a tool that (as we will keep hammering away at) you must keep locked up in the toolbox until you hit age 60.

Real Diversification

As we experienced the downturns of 2008 and 2020, and as we walked with clients in the years between, we gained some clarity about what true diversity looks like. People who weather economic storms have some things in common. Everyone can learn from and use these principles to make smart choices and guard against financial uncertainty when those economic cycles inevitably hit a low point.

These are the building blocks we use as core principles in our financial planning:

1. Owning and controlling streams of cash flow that continue to come in when the economy is down. We will discuss our Seven Sources of Residual Income at length later in the book. Sources of residual income, especially owning a business, creating intellectual property, and owning real property (real estate) as an investment are ways of creating cash flow that hedge against financial market instability.

2. Holding investments that are countercorrelated to economic crashes. This would be investments like gold, paid off real estate, cash value life insurance, and fixed, indexed income or income annuities.

When Do You Hit Time Freedom?

What is the end goal of financial planning? Simply put, it is when your income exceeds your expenses and you no longer must work for that money to come in. It is also based on investment projections that your money and thus your income won't run out. For most of us, that income is a combination of things. We don't want to worry about how we are going to pay our bills. Again, it's about income and options. We want to have the money and the ability to do the things we want to do. We want to enjoy things like travel, dining out, and entertainment without feeling like it is costing us our future. In short, we want to be comfortable and not worried about how we're going to pay to stay comfortable.

The goal is time freedom. That is, the freedom to live the life and do the things we want to do all the time and still have income to live on. That's what we are hoping for when we put money into an IRA or 401(k). The problem with these plans is that you can't meaningfully access that money until you're 59-and-a-half. These are sold to us as an instrument that keeps us from spending away our retirement. And there is some validity to this. Savings rates are historically low. We are a society that tends to spend more than we earn, from individuals to families, right on through to state and federal government.

People who accumulate and keep wealth do not rely on their 401(k) alone to manage some far off "retirement." They create what we call *Now Money* and leverage that in many ways. Maybe it is through owning a multi-family apartment, starting a business, or owning a franchise.

But think of the millionaire next door. That's what we want for you. Many years ago, we partnered together to form Uncommon Wealth Partners with this goal in mind, to help people leverage their Now Money in ways that complement their retirement savings accounts while increasing cash flow and net worth.

Growth of the Middle Class and the Invention of Retirement

Time freedom, financial freedom, or retirement income is a new concept for a large portion of humankind. For 5,000 years, there was no such thing as a retirement plan unless you were a king or part of the ruling class. Nobody lived long enough to retire. In pretty much every culture, there were a few people who had the money and power to live lives of leisure. That was the extent of time freedom.

Then, a merchant class arose. It was not a huge group of people, but between the poor and the aristocracy were shopkeepers, etc. Still, life expectancy was such that people tended to keel over at their shop desk at a fairly early age.

Enter the medical advances and economic expansion of the 20th century. A version of social security was created in Germany in 1896 because the younger citizens were struggling to find jobs and the older generation wouldn't stop working. So they introduced the first form of social security to help the older generation stop working to make way for the younger class. Then during the Great Depression in the 1930s, we in the U.S. found ourselves in a similar situation. Laws were written that led to our current Social Security legislation, which made 65 the retirement age at a time when the average life expectancy was 61.

So, for nearly 5,000 years of documented history, there was no social construct or legislation designed to provide income from a government-run program.

Early Forms of Retirement—The Three-Legged Stool

The original construct of retirement income planning was predicated on a version of the proverbial three-legged stool. This three-legged stool consisted of the three pillars of retirement: pensions, social security, and personal savings and/or investments. For a while, the combination of the first two legs made up a large portion of most Americans' retirement income in the form of pensions and social security.

Enter the IRA and 401(k), added in the 1970s as corporate pensions were raided and the burden of retirement passed from the company to the individual. The concept of an individual retirement fund was created because Wall Street started raiding corporate pensions and needed something to replace them with. That's why fewer people have pensions. We have all seen how the pension money dries up when a company hits hard times.

Let that sink in. What we think of as financial planning is a century-old experiment, and a large portion of that was developed after 1970.

But this whole system assumes we all want to plug away for the company until we hit retirement age. Then and only then can we do what we want to with our time.

That's a broken system.

But for argument's sake, let's just look at what we have come to think of as the typical trajectory. We work at a job, squirrel some money away in a 401(k) with, hopefully, an employer match or an IRA, and rely on social security to cover the gaps.

One thing that financial planners of all stripes understand is that the social safety-net of Social Security cannot be relied upon to provide what it has for most Americans up to this point. From its inception to the early 2000s, social security for most Americans was over 50% of their monthly retirement income. The system is already largely insolvent as our government has spent the lion's share of the funds that are withheld in taxes. More money is being sent out than collected for social security right now.

Looking at the construct of retirement income in the context of the three-legged stool, what we are shouting from the rooftops is that the old way of planning for retirement is broken for younger generations. Two of the three legs are being chopped out with pensions being eliminated and social security filing strategies being reduced. There is the potential for the government to move the full retirement age (FRA) of eligibility back for those under the age of 55. The Baby Boomers are already beginning to put a strain on the depleted system. Add to that, and what you will be able to draw from Social Security does not add up to the lifestyle most of us want at any age. Social Security may be around in 20 years, but it most certainly won't account for more than 50% of your desired retirement income. That is why you need to look at owning assets that produce cash flow as other ways to build wealth to complement your retirement savings.

Inflation and the Fed

We know that the government and the social programs of Social Security, Medicare, and Medicaid are at the point where more money is going out than is coming in. When you combine that with our federal debt that on average has been growing over $1 trillion annually, our government is spending way more than it is collecting.

So how do we pay for all this? The Federal Reserve helps us pay for all of this because our President and Congress gave them the power to print the currency in 1913. Since then, our national debt has ramped up and the value of the dollar has lost over 99% of its purchasing power.

Inflation is the silent killer of your savings. It's why we are so adamant that you look at the Seven Sources of Residual Income and structure assets that produce current cash flow that can offset inflationary effects.

Having the dollar lose 99% sounds ridiculous, but take a closer look. In 1913, one ounce of gold was worth $20. In 2020, one ounce of gold is worth nearly $2,000. When the U.S. was founded and our currency system was set up, our currency was backed by gold. For nearly 130 years until 1913, the United States grew in a fairly consistent manner having no real inflation and no income taxes outside of the Civil War.

That all changed in 1913 with the introduction of not only the Federal Reserve handling our money supply, but also with the introduction of Income Taxes to pay for World War I. The problem was they never went away.

We can bring this concept closer to home. Think about the first time you rode your bike to the gas station or grocery store and bought a candy bar. How much did it cost? When we were kids, it was around 45 cents. Now, when you go to the convenience store, you buy your kids a smaller Snickers bar, and it costs nearly $1.30. That is inflation, and when you stop working, it has a more profound impact on your wealth and purchasing power.

The Uncommon Path Forward

It's a complicated world out there. We don't want you to wait until you are a certain age to live out your dreams and hope your 401(k) is in good enough shape to allow for a comfortable retirement.

Business and real estate are great at hedging inflation risk for the owner because they can pass that cost on to the consumer. That is why we advocate the Seven Sources of Residual Income, because they are great tools and hedges against inflation. They provide you with a mechanism to increase your income over time to fight inflation.

Many times, our clients want to know what we are doing with our own money. Are we eating our own cooking? The answer is yes. Not only do we help you with your Uncommon Wealth Path, but we are on one as well.

So how do we take the principles of wealth-building outside retirement accounts and the stock market and teach others to build them into a cohesive, holistic planning process based on their strengths and capital?

How do you invest in yourself since you are your best asset? How do you organize your capital and your mind to invest in more things you can control and understand, but more importantly have more fun with and create the life you want to live now?

Throughout the book, we'll be sharing not only the principles we've been learning and teaching, but we'll be sharing the stories of people we've met along the way who have started down the Uncommon Path.

Let's get to it!

A Glimpse Down the Uncommon Path:

Jared Van Cleave - The Real Estate Agent

Real estate is one of the most powerful sources of residual income. There are so many ways to do it, and there are many ways to dip your toes in it to see how it suits you. Our first case study had the advantage of knowing real estate right out of the gate. What he didn't know was that it could be such a powerful engine for his personal and family goals.

Jared is a realtor who came to us with earnings that year well above his normal annual income. He wondered if he should invest in the stock market or in rental properties.

We invited him to do the math and model out the numbers. We

looked at a stock portfolio on one hand. Then we asked him if he felt owning and managing real estate in the city where he was selling real estate would help or hurt his business. We knew the answer. It would help his business.

Then we looked at the expected returns of the stock market versus owning and managing rental properties. What he soon found out was the cash flow from real estate was nearly double the stock market, plus it enhanced his primary source of income as a realtor. Owning properties gave him a deeper understanding of the local market, and the people renting from him often went on to purchase homes as well. Residual income from rentals plus profits from selling real estate allowed him to expand his portfolio faster because they worked together.

Finally, we asked him what he would learn from owning and managing properties versus investing in the stock market. He knew he would learn a lot not only about real estate, but also about himself if he took the route of investing in real estate. He would learn very little if anything by putting his money in a hands-off stock portfolio.

This is important, so we want to highlight this here. In a caring way, we provided a framework for him to prove his investment thesis and address questions about how to handle the risk and potential pit-falls of owning and operating rental properties. Through the process, he had an answer and strategy to address every question. As we compared that to investing in the stock market, it was clear he had very little knowledge of, or the passion for, investing in a stock portfolio.

Everything you do outside of leaving money in the bank involves risk, but if you understand it and know how to mitigate it as part of a plan, you are way ahead of the game. When you are operating in your sphere of excellence, understanding, and passion, that is truly when the risk is lowered because you know what you are doing and can capitalize on that knowledge.

Managing multiple rental properties and handling the seasonality of selling real estate in the Midwest required sitting on a lot of cash that wasn't really doing anything other than being liquid in the bank. Implementing the Uncommon Banking system (which we will touch on in Chapter 7) created another asset that allowed Jared's money to work. It secured a death benefit, tax protection, and compound interest, all while being liquid to help fund and pay off rental properties conventionally financed at the bank. Again, this acted as another asset that was pulling in the same direction as his real estate and rental income.

Uncommon Wealth Tactics:

A New Tool

Here is a tool that we call the Uncommon Financial Dashboard, and we hope it will help give you a clear picture of your Uncommon Path. Throughout this book we will highlight each section, how to fill it out, and why it is important in this journey.

You can create your Uncommon Financial Dashboard for free at **www.uncommonwealth.com/financial-dashboard**, and it looks like this:

Clear Focus

Ideal/Realistic Financial Freedom Date _____

Age: _____ Age at Financial Freedom: _____

Monthly Financial Freedom Number_____

Projected Monthly Income at Financial Freedom Date

_____

Sources of Income Projected at Financial Freedom Date

_____

Again, to create an Uncommon Financial Dashboard you can edit and print, go to www.uncommonwealth.com/financial-dashboard. Because you bought this book, you get free access. Your Uncommon Financial Dashboard will be a powerful resource, helping you organize and simplify your message, and you'll use it again and again. With the Uncommon Financial Dashboard tool, you will be able to see your goals and dreams on a single page in relation to where you are investing your money and whether those are aligned to support one another and hold you accountable to an actionable path forward.

It starts with a Clear Focus. Just like a good marksman practices with a clear and defined target, we also need to define what we want to accomplish.

Ideal/Realistic Financial Freedom Date: The date you want to be living off the income of your investments. Think of the day you want to have enough income to cover how you live your day-to-day life.

Ages: The age you and your spouse are currently.

Financial Freedom Monthly Number: The amount of money that needs to come in for you to live comfortably each month. Many people look at this number as the amount that is coming in from the job that they currently have, or how much is hitting their bank account each month. Think about if the money that you currently work for was coming in automatically. That is your Monthly Financial Freedom Number. Your number might be higher than what is currently coming in, but this is to give you a baseline of what you want your monthly number to be. If you don't have a target, you most likely will never achieve it. Lastly, don't think about your current debt load, just think about the number you want to be coming in each month. And remember the higher this number is, the harder you will most likely have to work for it.

Projected Monthly Income at Financial Freedom Date: A dollar today is worth less than a dollar 20 years ago. Therefore, we need to account for inflation in your plan as well. We like to use 2% for this calculation. To calculate this follow these four steps:

1. Take the *year* you want to be financially free minus the *year* it is currently, and that will give you how many years you have to become financially free. For this example, let's use 15 years.

2. Then take your Monthly Financial Freedom Number and multiply that number by 12 so you know how much money a year you want to live off of. For this, let's say your number is $8,000 per month. So 8,000 x 12 = $96,000.

3. Run a Google search for a compounding interest calculator, and use the number from Step 2 as your initial investment (96,000). Then enter zero for your monthly contribution, and your length of years should be the value from Step 1 (15 years). For estimated interest rate, we like to use 2 percent. After all the numbers are in, hit calculate. That number will be an annual estimate of what you will need when you want to be financially free.

4. Take whatever number that is (in this example it is $129,203.36) and divide that by 12 to get your Projected Monthly Income at financial freedom number, **$10,766.95**.

Sources of Income Projected at Financial Freedom Date: How many ways are you projecting to be receiving money at the date you want to be financially free? This will be just a number.

Here is an example once you are done:

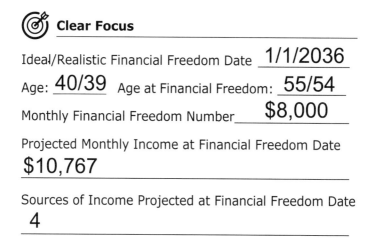

Clear Focus

Ideal/Realistic Financial Freedom Date 1/1/2036

Age: 40/39 Age at Financial Freedom: 55/54

Monthly Financial Freedom Number $8,000

Projected Monthly Income at Financial Freedom Date
$10,767

Sources of Income Projected at Financial Freedom Date
4

We will keep unpacking sections of this Uncommon Financial Dashboard in each chapter.

CHAPTER 3

Uncommon Mindset:
You Are Your Best Asset

As children, when we are asked what we want to be when we grow up, the sky is the limit. We talk about what we love or what excites us. Maybe it's being an astronaut, an actor, or an athlete.

Children aren't worried about what people earn doing those jobs. It seems like an awesome way to spend your time, so why wouldn't they want to do that? Adults ask children this question because we love their enthusiasm and their sense of unbridled possibility.

Children believe in themselves. They don't have the language or experience to put this into words, but they understand doing something that is exciting. And what do we do when our kids come to us and say, "Hey, I want to play soccer!"? We invest in them. We say, "Let's sign you up for a team where you can learn and have a coach." We invest in our children's latest passion: band, football, baseball, singing, theatre, dance, you name it. We find places where they can be coached and learn to excel.

Then somewhere along the way, the child drops that sport or gets a part-time job to earn some money, and that unbridled sense of possibility starts to wane.

Adults may love to hear the aspirations of kids, but we are also the ones who quickly tamp down those aspirations. Sure, part of this is just cold reality. Both children and adults learn that not everyone has the skills or the passion to keep training to become a top athlete. There are only a few astronaut gigs to go around. Hollywood is a tough town.

But it goes further than that. We're eventually told in so many words that we need to be realistic. We need to be practical.

Being practical is the societal norm. A norm that says we need to go to school for the purpose of finding a good job with good benefits, then work and save money for a someday that is always just out of reach.

That kind of mindset is making the anti-depressant industry a ton of money.

When you are told to temper your dreams, to settle down and follow the path that everyone around you is following, that seems like the only option available. We settle for the practical and sensible path.

What is Work?

The biggest mindset shift we help people with comes in their view of work. So many people view earning as doing one thing for an employer. There are so many ways to make money. Later in the book, we're going to explore the Seven Sources of Residual Income in detail.

But for now, let's keep it simple. You have so many options for making money beyond your day job. Maybe it's real estate or writing that book you've been meaning to write (royalties). Maybe it's building some kind of business that someone else can manage day-to-day.

The point is, work and earning money are so much more than the place you go to earn a paycheck. Think about how much money you are making the company you work for. Why would that be any different if you went out and started your own gig? We are not saying you will replace your income in the first year, but could you embark on a path to control your destiny and live in your sweet spot?

Spinning Plates

Have you ever seen a plate-spinning performer? It's where the performer takes a long stick and spins a plate on top of that stick, and the gyroscopic stability keeps the plate from falling. Then the performer adds another stick and another plate and so on and so forth until they have multiple spinning plates.

Spinning plates takes some skill. To get one plate spinning on top of a stick is admirable. But imagine a performer spinning two plates, each on opposite ends of the stage. It would be fun to watch, but a real challenge for the performer. Traditional financial planning has you acting like this performer. That's what it's like when we spin one plate—managing our monthly expenses—and then spin another plate across the stage of contributions to a 401(k) or retirement plan. Wouldn't it make more sense for the performer to start spinning a second plate very near to the first plate?

Spinning the second plate right next to the first is like starting to save an emergency fund and put capital together to invest. Something that is safe and liquid.

Starting to save for retirement when you are just starting out doesn't really help you now and could take your focus and energy away from investing in your passions and gifts. Imagine this: instead of the third plate you spin, instead of contributing to a 401(k) to get the match, you invested that same capital into a rental property as a down payment, but another person came on stage to spin that third plate for you in the form of a property manager or renter?

The Uncommon Formula

A different way of financial planning starts with an Uncommon approach. It starts with understanding what you are uniquely gifted at and what you enjoy. Instead of what you want to do later in life, what do you want and think about right now?

That's the Uncommon Mindset.

So how do you get there? We spend a lot of time just listening and asking questions. These questions are our way of truly hearing our clients, understanding what their goals are, and helping them get there as soon as possible. People have dreams now, not just for when they hit age 65.

Our approach helps you unleash the Uncommon Mindset by understanding three key principles:

- **YOU ARE YOUR BEST ASSET**—You are made in a unique way, with gifts and a purpose that, when aligned, bring out your passion.

- **ORGANIZE YOUR MONEY TO INVEST IN YOUR PASSION**—This is about maintaining a focus on your purpose and goals in life and how money can help you achieve those goals, rather than focusing on money itself.

- **MONETIZE YOUR PASSION**—There are so many ways to make money from what makes you unique and passionate. In working with clients, we highlight those business models or ideas that are synergistic with your passions and skillsets.

Mindset Shift #1:

You Are Your Best Asset

What does it mean to believe that you are your best asset? How do you get yourself back to that childlike capacity to believe you can do anything?

As a child, everything is a new adventure, and we haven't developed major fears, misconceptions, wounds, or failures. Anything seems possible, and we are interested and curious in the world around us. We are purposeful in trying new things, being coached, and improving our skills. As we try new things, our passions ramp up and we get excited about new possibilities and opportunities.

Soon enough, wonder gives way to lessons adults teach us about life—some well-meaning and some not. We're confronted with words and phrases like failure, hate, comparison, we can't afford that, or don't waste your time on that. Well-meaning or not, these lessons stunt our ability to maintain that childlike mindset.

What it really boils down to is that nobody really shows you how to invest in your ideas, and more importantly, in yourself and your ability to accomplish those ideas. Generating income and conquering the obstacles that come up and stand in your way is not something that is taught in school. The path is slowly paved for you to get a job and get in line. Soon, the flame within fades.

But understand this:

Your hopes and dreams for the life you want are the core of the Uncommon Mindset.

No one is going to put more money in your pocket than yourself. Your ability to generate income is a powerful thing, and an asset worth protecting. But the path to earning that money should ideally come from that place of wonder and passion.

Mindset is all about the messages we tell ourselves and the people who surround us. If you don't believe in your own potential, that is going to be a roadblock to an Uncommon mind.

Who are the people who are most influential in your life? Do they believe in you? All too often, we see people who have been told they won't amount to anything. If you are surrounding yourself with people who tell you with words or actions to "stay in your lane," those are not the ones to pay any attention to.

This is a path that takes courage. But you have that within you. We like to help people flesh out what they want their life to be like now, and then we help them organize their money to facilitate those decisions. When this is done as part of a financial plan, they don't feel like they're stealing from their future.

We like to say, "Do what you love, and you will never want to quit."

Finding a Mentor

The most critical activity in keeping our goals and visions alive is mentorship. Mentorship is different from coaching. When you sign up for the local soccer team, you are paired up with a coach. Who you have as a coach is just the luck of the draw. But sometimes a parent will invest a bit extra and learn about the coaches before just plopping their child on a random team. That is more intentional. The parents are saying, "Hey, you are talented. Let's be strategic in this next decision."

A mentor is someone you respect and who is in a stage of life that you aspire to be. They have accomplished something that you are trying to do yourself, and their wisdom and knowledge would help you on your journey. Mentorship is a two-way street. Mentors have a vested interest in seeing you accomplish your goals. They see potential in you and are willing to prove it with their time and knowledge. They also expect you to respect their time and do the work they are telling you to do.

In sports, it's easy to see if you are the next LeBron James or not, because in sports the court is the great equalizer. Can you play or not? In life, things get blurry and grey. How does the next Bill Gates, Mark Cuban, or Martha Stewart develop? There isn't an Amateur Athletic Union (AAU) league for starting your own business or developing a real estate portfolio. If you don't have parents with resources or a mindset of personal growth, development, and capital to invest, you may never know there is a different way to invest or build a business. Finding a mentor who has what you want is critical to unlocking the vision and dream you may hold. Mentorship is the cheat code to life. It allows you to download the wisdom and avoid the pitfalls the person made themselves, so you can achieve results faster.

Mindset Shift #2:

Organize Your Money to Invest in Your Passion

So much of what society calls wealth-building is storing up for an emergency or maxing out a 401(k) for some later time. That is the all-too-common path.

Here is the common equation most of us are used to when it comes to money: we defer 6-10% of our income before we get paid into a company-sponsored retirement plan. We also leave two to three months' income in a savings account for an emergency or a rainy day.

That's too often how the financial plan is put into place. Most financial advisors approach you with the mindset that they are your best asset and that you need them and their shiny stock market returns to get ahead. It simply isn't true. They are solving for retirement first. Retirement is when you stop doing what you are currently doing and start doing what you are supposedly passionate about.

What's wrong with that picture? The plan should start with you. As your own best asset, what do you want out of life? If you had resources, what would you want your money to do for you right now? When you shift to the mindset that you are your best asset, you are focused on the here and now. In Chapter 4, we will start laying out the groundwork to organize your money to invest in your passion.

Clients are surprised by our approach, which is basically to ask you questions, understand your goals, and then see how we can move you toward your goals sooner rather than later. It doesn't seem as safe as putting money away and not looking at it until you are 60 because that is what everyone else is telling you to do.

When considering yourself as your own greatest asset and thinking about what you want your money to do for you, a mindset shift takes place. You are willing not just to think back with nostalgia about a childhood filled with dreams. You realize that you have the skills and the drive right now to organize your money to invest in your passions. This is far from child's play. It is the drumbeat that is putting you on the Uncommon Path. Our focus is on investing in things you know and control that generate income or cash flow now. If we help you increase your monthly income by $1,000 a month right now, that will also help you later. This mindset shift from thinking about your retirement account balance to thinking about your cash-flow is the definition of retirement. Retirement is all about living on the cash-flow from your assets rather than working for a living. Practicing that mindset now, helps you later.

Mindset Shift #3:

Monetize Your Passion

As we mentioned above, when you boil it down, the real problem is that we are taught to ignore our passions and head down that path everyone else is walking, instead of focusing on how to monetize our passion. If you love baking cookies when you are 16, unless you seek out a mentor, a local baker, or get serious about business advice, chances are nobody is going to really show you how to monetize cookie-baking and make it a viable path for your future. If the people in your life think you would be better suited going to college and working for someone else, they are probably much less enthusiastic about encouraging you to own your own bakery.

Why is the default mindset to get a job? We hear the principle that when you are younger, you can take more risks because you have more time to recover from losses, yet all the financial advice focuses on risk in terms of a portfolio you can't touch until you retire. When you are young, that is the time to take risks with your passion, not your retirement portfolio.

What if the default was investing in yourself and your ideas at a younger age and trying to make that work before going to get a job? If you take a risk and invest in a crazy idea, you will still be able to get a job if you fail.

This is why we are so passionate about the Seven Sources of Residual Income, because there are so many paths that you can take not only to make money, but also to pursue what you are passionate about and thrive. Pursuing Uncommon Wealth provides you a career path that you can control, innovate, and be passionate about. So many people are giving financial advice, but it is one-dimensional. Dave Ramsey focuses on debt reduction, but doesn't show you ways to build wealth beyond the stock market. Tony Robbins is starting to talk about finances. So much of it is centered around the stock market, which isn't how he created his wealth. Robert Kiyosaki focuses a lot on business and real estate but lacks the fundamentals of how to get there or get started.

How do you take the tools, principles, and models the wealthy use and build a cohesive financial plan that excites you, gives you more control, and helps you build the life you want to live? That is the task at hand as you start to monetize your passion.

Making the Shift

When you think of yourself as your own best asset, the possibilities open. You think about everything differently when you understand and believe in your own potential.

That is our most profound desire for you. Now, let's look at a case study to help you reinforce this new mindset.

A Glimpse Down the Uncommon Path:

**Ian and Christina Nelson-Johnson –
The Psyched Psychologist and the Pumped-Up Yogi**

The Uncommon Life is not all rainbows and unicorns. Sometimes we face challenges that seem insurmountable in the moment. Mike Tyson used to say, "Everyone has a plan until you get punched in the face."

That's what happened with our next couple. On their way toward a perfect life together in Oregon, Ian and Christina faced several personal and professional challenges. They made the decision to face the storm and chase a dream rather than put it off for years to come.

After studying for years to become a psychologist, a paperwork snafu cost Ian a dream post-doctoral job at a local university. It was devastating. They had moved to Oregon for him to finish up his studies. They both loved the outdoors and were looking forward to getting married and living in the picturesque Northwest.

Now what? There was no immediate and magic answer. After a year of sticking around Oregon and kind of floundering, it was a scary time for them. They felt like several doors were shut in Oregon, so they decided to make their way back home to Iowa.

After all this, Ian did get the paperwork straightened out and is now a licensed clinical psychologist. We got to know them when he and Phillip were playing the epic sport of Roundnet/Spikeball on the same team.

On Christina and Ian's return to Iowa, they thought that maybe they could shoot for a 10-year plan for Ian to open his own counseling practice. In the face of it, this seemed like a pragmatic goal. They didn't have much in savings. They had moved twice in a short time, and Ian had lost his job in the middle of all that. They wanted to face these obstacles with eyes wide open.

But as we helped them look at their situation, we thought a 10-year time frame seemed a little bit arbitrary. Why not get that process moving sooner? While they were thinking about all of this, Christina had become very interested in yoga and decided that she wanted to become an instructor.

Why not combine those passions into one practice? That's just what they did. Now they are running the Ames Mind Body Center together, offering individual therapy, group therapy, and yoga.

Ian works with people from all walks of life. His work focuses on the following areas: men's issues, relationship distress, trauma, depression, gender identity, anxiety, grief, family of origin concerns, spirituality, and identity concerns.

Christina is a yoga instructor who has now practiced and taught yoga all over the world—from a college class in Portland, Oregon, to a basement studio in Amsterdam, Netherlands, to an ashram outside Sydney, Australia.

How did they make this big leap? When they came to us, they were clinging to a Roth IRA like a life raft on the Titanic. It was all the wealth they had managed to save. We get that. Most of our clients come to us having been taught never to touch that Later Money they've been carefully putting away.

But we encouraged them to do the unthinkable. Why not cash out the Roth IRA and use that as seed money for this business they were dreaming of? Because you don't cash out your IRA before you turn 60, Bryan and Phillip, that's why!

Ok, we understand. That's the message you hear over and over. But we see time and again that a faster way to grow wealth is to build a business and create another asset—another income stream—to help pay debts and move ahead. Their business was started with less than $10,000 cash. Ian started seeing patients at night after his day job was over. It went very quickly as he worked hard and built his practice. Christina helped handle a lot of the business operations and setup.

They used the extra income to purchase their first home, light years ahead of when they thought they would be able to buy one. They found the perfect property with an additional guest bedroom that they now rent out on Airbnb. This is their fourth stream of income. They did all of this in less than 12 months, with a baby on the way, starting with less than $10,000.

Again, opening their own business leveraging his psychology degree and license was synergistic to his gifts and passions and aligned with his future goals. Combining that with her passion for yoga added another income stream and outlet to be creative and design their life on their terms. Now they have brought on additional therapists to the business, allowing them to help even more people in less than 12 short months. This was something they thought was going to take 10 years to do, but they did it in less than one.

Now, let's take a step back. We know it is super controversial to cash out a Roth IRA of $11,000, but let's look at the math. They had put most of that money into the Roth IRA, so there weren't a lot of penalties or taxes due. The counseling business is now generating $1,000 a week in profit off that $11,000 decision. Not to mention the income from yoga and now Airbnb. What is the return on their investment versus leaving the money in the stock market? Even if the money was to double in the stock market, it wouldn't have helped them open a business, double their income, or buy a house for their growing family. That is the power of leveraging Now Money for today's dreams and tomorrow's needs.

This is the Uncommon Path, and they have embodied all of it with open arms and a strong work ethic. They found a way to unite their passion for helping others and building community, all while gaining control of their life on their terms.

If you want to hear the full story of their journey, check out the podcast here: **https://www.uncommonwealth.com/podcasts/ian-christina-nelson-johnson**

Uncommon Wealth Tactics:

Next Section of the Uncommon Financial Dashboard:

🪪 Investor Profile

Investment Objective_____

Risk Tolerance _____

Investment Objective:

Knowing your Investment Objective is helpful for us as we partner with you to try to achieve Uncommon Wealth. Here are the categories that can help you identify your investment objective:

Capital Preservation—Not wanting loss of your principal on your asset/investment

Income—Asset/Investment solely focused on income without concern for the asset/investment growing in value

Growth & Income—Wanting more income specifically for asset/investment growth

Growth—Wanting to grow without concern for income

Aggressive Growth—High-risk strategy designed for significant growth

Speculation—Very high-risk strategy that seeks maximum gain and potential total loss

Risk Tolerance is determined by your personality, and other factors:

High—I am expecting extreme ups and downs in my asset/investment

Moderate—I am ok with moderate ups and downs in my asset/investment

Low—I want to limit my downside as much as possible in my asset/investment

EXAMPLE:

Investor Profile

Investment Objective___Growth and Income___

Risk Tolerance ___Moderate___

CHAPTER 4

Where Are You Now and Where Do You Want to Be?

Life is thrilling. Life is scary. Life is unpredictable. Life is precious, and it's all we have. Remember, life is so much more than what is in your bank account.

When we meet with potential clients, they are always, *always* surprised that we don't start the conversation asking about what's in their wallet or retirement plan.

Since we are trying to help people build an Uncommon Life, we start with the question, "What do you want your life to look like, right now and in the future?" We are trying to discern where they are currently, what their goals are for the future, and how to bridge the gap, all while taking into account their past experience, finances, and risk tolerance.

I (Phillip) love meeting with a potential client over coffee. They assume we will be taking a deep dive into their money situation. But I ask about their life, who they are, and what their story is. By the end of the conversation, I haven't even asked them about financial assets or spending habits. I just want to know who they are and what their attitude is about their current situation.

That is our starting point, and it never fails to surprise people.

Maybe you've heard the story of the three bricklayers. We came across this parable recently that illustrates the mindset necessary if you want to go down the Uncommon Path that can lead to Uncommon Wealth.

The Three Bricklayers

There are three bricklayers on a job site. A man walks up to the first bricklayer and asks him, "What are you doing?" The first bricklayer replied, "What does it look like I am doing? I am doing a job and laying bricks."

The man moves on to the next bricklayer and asks him what he is doing, and he says, "I am providing for my family and earning a living."

The man then went to the last bricklayer and asked him, "What are you doing?" The last bricklayer replied, "I am building an amazing cathedral for God's people."

What is the difference between these bricklayers? We believe it is a mindset. The first bricklayer had a very poor mindset when it came to doing his job every day. The next bricklayer may or may not enjoy his work every day, but he did have a purpose and that purpose was providing.

The third bricklayer's mindset is the most important to talk about. He had a vision that was bigger than himself. He had a sense of purpose and he took pride in it. We would argue that not only is he providing for his family by doing the work, but that he is also passionate while doing it. He has a vocation, not just a job.

We work with all three and don't judge people, no matter where they are. Sometimes a job needs to be done, and there is nothing wrong with that. This illustration is meant to help you make a quick and honest assessment of where you are and where you want to be. So, looking at the bricklayer analogy, which bricklayer do you identify with the most?

The process for working with all three is remarkably similar. The advice will change, though, depending on which bricklayer you are.

If you want to hear more on how we unpack the bricklayer analogy and general advice we give to each person, check out our Uncommon Life Podcast Episode 53.

https://www.uncommonwealth.com/podcasts/duocast-22/

What is Your Identity?

At first, people come to us because they want to plan for a better future. Often, they realize they need to get on track and they need some help in making that happen. Now, through our process and planning, we identify what root issues are truly holding them back from what they communicate they want. When those things can be identified, we can work through those together, and when they can align their money and resources to support that change, it is powerful.

We recently met a gentleman who wanted to retire. He had met with five financial advisors before us. The interesting thing about this man was that he had plenty of money, and all the other advisors knew it. The planning was honestly pretty easy. It usually is when you have a lot of money. The challenge he faced was that he wanted to retire but couldn't. The problem wasn't his money, the problem was how his identity was wrapped up in his money.

He wanted to be retired, but because his money was his legacy and his identity, he wasn't going to trust anyone with that. Our plan for this gentleman solved his issues for retirement income, market swings, inflation, taxes, death, and the possibility of a nursing home.

More importantly, he realized his true identity was that of a husband, father, and a grandfather. Our work together helped him understand he wouldn't be remembered for what he left behind, but the way he spent the time he had left.

There is a disconnect between this level of hoping and dreaming and traditional financial planning. It can get transactional pretty fast. But when you seek financial advice, you don't want to feel like your advisor is just steering you toward a product. The feeling we had when we were working for large financial service companies got a little too close for comfort.

You want your money to help fund and invest in what you are excited and passionate about. You want to be known, heard, and seen in your best light. You want to be focused beyond yourself, like the third bricklayer. Even in retirement, you still want to be in a position of strength, passion, and community.

Once we have heard your story and understand who you are and what you are passionate about, that is when we feel comfortable starting to understand the money side of things. Money is a tool, and we want to make sure that when we give advice, we are directing your money to invest in your goals.

For example, we meet lots of couples who seriously want to retire before they are 60, but a large portion of the money they have saved to this point is in a company-sponsored retirement plan. Based on the way the laws and tax code govern those plans, it is hard to retire before 60 if that is your primary mechanism for saving and investing.

We want to stop focusing on money and start focusing on the things you want the money to do for you. With a deep dive into who you are and what makes you tick, we can become an advocate for you.

You can achieve your goals sooner than you think.

Stop Talking About Retirement and Start Talking About Living

"What do you want retirement to look like?" is a pretty standard question you get from financial planners. We're doing what we're doing precisely because we hate that question. It puts the process backwards.

It all comes back to our core question. What do you love to do, and when would you stop doing that? If you are in a similar position to the first bricklayer, you are not doing what you love or are passionate about, and things need to change more quickly. If you are the second bricklayer, your work may not have you at a breaking point, but it is certainly not something you imagine doing forever. If you are the third bricklayer, you couldn't imagine doing anything else, and the idea of slowing down is not your mindset.

It's our opinion and experience that most people want to end up like the third bricklayer. It just might be in a different vocation than what you are in now. Some of the skills and talents you possess are being used currently, but they aren't being applied in a way that excites and motivates you.

When you love what you do, you never want to stop. Our approach is to totally reframe the question of retirement. What if retirement was not some set age where you stop doing a job? What if you could get to that point sooner than you think? What if your life could be such that you could do what you love and the cash flow was there for you to do that? That would be pretty great, right?

And when we get to this level—the level of dreams that maybe you haven't expressed out loud to anyone but your closest friends and family members; when you talk to us about what you love and your goals for life both now and in the future, that's when we can start talking about the money.

This is the exciting starting point of a plan that is potentially life-altering. One of our favorite examples of this was when we met a woman who owned her own dental practice. We sat down for lunch and she stated that she was interviewing other advisors as she wanted to pick the "right one" for her. We proceeded to have an amazing conversation over lunch. All we did was ask about her, about her practice, where it was currently, where she saw it going in the future, how many kids she had, and a lot more questions about her life. As we finished lunch, she asked, "When are we going to start talking about my money?" We replied that we had been talking about her money the whole time.

Two weeks later, she called us back saying she had a big influx of money coming in. What did we think she should do with it? Because we knew her, what was important, where she wanted to go, and what she valued, we gave her advice. She said, "That is exactly what I thought." Often, people know what they want to do with the money, but they want to know it is aligned with a bigger plan that works for them.

Most advisors already have a plan for you before you sit down with them. That plan is to have you invest as much as possible into accounts that they can get paid from. That is the advice they offer to clients. They want you to see them as an invaluable asset in planning for the future.

A preconceived plan is not enough. Helping clients figure out their talents and helping them build a financial plan around that is the stuff we love about what we do. And if you have not guessed, our faith informs how we do business. There is a spiritual component to conversations about money. God has designed each of us in a unique way. What we try to help clients do is embrace that uniqueness and then invest in it.

We value people, their experiences (good and bad), their gifts, and helping them understand their "why." Our approach is about empowering people to start dreaming again while asking as many questions as needed to clarify and bring focus to their future.

How to Replace a Paycheck and Benefits with Residual Income

In the economic climate we live in, it is becoming abundantly clear that a paycheck and benefits are not a sure path to safety and security. With so many living paycheck to paycheck at every level of the economic spectrum, there has to be a better way to build wealth than the bill of goods we've been sold about a good job with benefits and a 401(k) contribution. Think about the first bricklayer and if the first and only place he starts saving is his 401(k). That traps him longer into the life of just doing a job. When he does figure out the next step to take, it will be a lot more frightening because he doesn't have anything to really fall back on financially.

So when we talk to people about their hopes and dreams, the money side of the conversation centers on cash flow and assets. How can we help you build cash flow to finance the life of your dreams? In our own experience of working at jobs in the industry (believe us, we've been there with that first bricklayer), we found out that for the most part, traditional financial planning is focused on taking money from you for later, not increasing your cash flow now.

It's all about guiding you gently into a future where you trade the paycheck and benefits to living off your investments.

Traditional financial planning is about creating a steady fixed income in retirement. Yet at the same time, "fixed income" carries a lot of baggage. Traditional financial planning promises an approximation of the lifestyle you've become accustomed to with this fixed income. But who knows if that's how it will work out?

Again, if the end game is lifelong sustained residual income, then why not start practicing that right now? If you have never generated residual income on your own until retirement, it is very hard to trust relying on your investments to retire. It's just hard to know where the money will come from and whether it will run out. For instance, people who have owned rental property, a business, or had a side hustle making between $500 and $1,000 a month on their own outside their paycheck are a lot more mentally and emotionally ready because they have done it before.

Those things in life that we want to be good at take practice. Oddly, what we are saying is to start practicing retirement right now. And what we see over and over is that as people do that, they like it. They feel more in control of their finances, not less. They feel more empowered than if they were just investing in the stock market through a 401(k) or brokerage account.

Here's one of the many awesome things about the Uncommon Wealth philosophy: you don't need to settle for a "fixed" income now or whenever you decide to retire. A focus on cash flow means you have ongoing residual income streams. So covering your basic expenses becomes the baseline that you can grow from there.

There's no reason to stop growing your residual income after "retirement."

What Does Wealth Mean to You?

Wealth is a subjective concept. In helping people build the life they want now, some of our questions are focused on what wealth means to them.

You may have read an article or seen a meme on Facebook to the effect that many American families are a $500 emergency away from financial hardship. In other words, when you are living paycheck to paycheck and your car breaks down, that quickly turns into a crisis.

Yet part of those expenses is often a $500 contribution to a retirement plan that is decades away from being utilized. We know the lives of families would be dramatically changed with something as simple but as life-changing as an extra $500 a month.

Are the decisions you are making with your money keeping you stuck? Be honest with yourself and your loved ones. Are you satisfied where you are? If not, you may need to shift the way your money is being handled or invested to support a change. Often, people are concerned that change will compromise retirement in the future.

You can have both, and it can be even better than you might think.

So why keep contributing money monthly and socking it away for a change two to four decades away? This may seem prudent, but with a residual income approach instead of a traditional retirement plan approach, you can be doing both at the same time. It's not magic, and we'll be going in depth into some strategies to make your cash flow work exactly this way in Chapter 7.

Happy, Fulfilled, and Thriving

What if you could be happy, fulfilled, and thriving all at the same time? This is exactly why we start our process with getting to know people.

This is where you must be honest with yourself and what is driving your decision.

Are you doing what you thought you would be at this point? Are you happy and fulfilled in what you are doing now? Do you feel valued and purposeful with your time and talent?

What do you see yourself doing to be the third bricklayer?

A Glimpse Down the Uncommon Path:

The Passive Income Pastor

It's great to have good intentions, but you need the right advice and the right tools to really begin and amp up the journey down the Uncommon Wealth Path. Here's a great story about how real estate, intellectual property, and Uncommon Banking can put your good intentions to good use.

When this pastor first came to us, he talked a lot about his church and the struggles the whole church was having. It turns out he was using the Dave Ramsey curriculum with his congregation. We are not fans. We explained why we thought that curriculum was so damaging to him and the congregation. Dave Ramsey's philosophy of waiting to invest until all your debt is paid off limits your ability to leverage your talents today and other people's resources to help you increase your current cash flow. If the Uncommon Wealth creation is done well, it could help you pay off your debt faster while enjoying your life. Not only are you going to be more fulfilled, but you can also give more and potentially employ more.

In terms of his personal finance, he and his wife came to us with a Roth IRA, limited investment experience, and an appetite to please the Lord and lead his congregation. We showed him how to unlock the Roth IRA, but still earn on it with our Uncommon Banking Strategy, then borrow against that to buy his first rental property.

Again, we are not about get-rich-quick schemes, but it did allow them to hire people from their congregation to help remodel the new investment property. They saw the power of hiring people within their church and the immediate economic impact of investing now. It honestly was a bit of a struggle for them to get the investment property rented once the renovations were done. It was difficult finding that first tenant, costing them months of lost rent. But they stayed patient and diligent and were able to get the property rented.

Then he took things a step further. He happened to hear one of our podcasts where our guest, Mitch Matthews, told us the story of a woman making residual income from writing books. Our pastor client had always wanted to write a book. We met with him five months later, and that's when he told us about hearing the podcast—and how he went ahead and self-published a book through Amazon.

Next up, he called to tell us he and his wife were interested in the short-term rental market. They just launched their first Airbnb, achieving 90% occupancy in their first two months!

This pastor went from one capped, fixed salary and one source of income, to now having multiple streams of income in just three years. Was the better investment to pay off all their debt, or live creating wealth and leading by example? The other great thing about his real estate ventures was hiring people from his church like electricians, plumbers, and handymen to do a lot of the remodeling work.

The Passive Income Pastor now has real estate ventures and has published two books and counting. We call him that for his focus on passive income, but his faith, hard work, and passion are anything but passive.

Uncommon Wealth Tactics:

Documenting Your Goals and Visions

The common thread among those we have interviewed and coached is that they reach a point where they are uncomfortable enough with the status quo that they decide to change their future.

The Jumanji drumbeat inside is so strong, it cannot be ignored any longer. The drumbeat keeps getting louder and won't go away.

Being clear with what you value and want in your life is the first step in claiming you as your best asset. We mean crystal clear. Being specific about the things you value and the timeline you want to use will help you create a plan to achieve it.

The clearer you are, the easier it is to plan for, and the easier it is to lay out baby steps to achieve your goals. Often, we hear people's excuses in a vague sense, and when we work through obstacles with real numbers, they quickly realize their fear or worst-case scenario isn't as bad as they thought.

What are the tangible goals for your Uncommon Wealth? The clients we love to work with are the clients who have clear goals. To help you think through this, we use the acronym SMART. It's an idea attributed to Peter Drucker's Management by Objectives, although we have changed two of the letters (A and R) from Attainable to Actionable and Realistic to Radical based on the wisdom and work of Dr. Anthony Paustian and his writings detailing HARD Goals.

Specific—Clear objective so you know what you are working toward

Measurable—Something that can be objectively measured so you know when you have achieved your goal

Actionable—Something that can be started immediately

Radical—If there were no obstacles in your way what would you want?

Time Bound—Has a clear date by which it needs to be finished

Goals

Five Year

Three Year

One Year

After you are done, it should look something like this:

 Goals

Five Year
- Ben's LLC Valued at 300k
- 1.5 Net Worth
- 401k Balances 600k
- No student loans
- Mortgage paid down to 250k

Three Year
- Ben's LLC kicking off 4k mo
- 850k Net Worth
- No car debt
- Student loan $24,000

One Year
- Ben's LLC kicking off $1,000
- Susan get a promotion
- Go after Ben's Car debt

CHAPTER 5

The Uncommon Process: Getting to Where You Want to Be

Understanding who you are and what motivates you is the first step on the Uncommon Path, and we love to help people start down that road. Our clients come to us looking for advice on how to build a financial base that allows them to live a life that matches their gifts and aspirations.

To get there, you've got to have a process. We pride ourselves on a human approach that starts with a conversation that has nothing to do with what's in your bank account. But at the end of the day, money is a big part of facilitating those dreams, so it's time to put a plan in place.

Uncommon Goals and Defining Success

How are you building a path toward financial and time freedom? What does success mean to you? What would it take to meet your success goals? Beyond all the questions we ask is a path forward that we've been testing and refining over the past eight years and counting.

Like defining wealth, defining success is also subjective. We want to set up goals that will meet success under your terms.

So we ask people, "What would it look like to be successful in our relationship and building wealth over the next five years?" This is not our way of getting you to sign up for a five-year commitment to work with us. It's another way of drilling down to what really matters to you. It's a way of discovering where you're coming from and where you want to go.

Often when people are dreaming about something they would like to do, it's a front-burner interest. If they had the means, they would do it right away. Rather than sending a "slow down and cool your jets" message about waiting for some far-off retirement plan, we like to help people imagine what it would take to make that dream a reality right now.

We call this the Get to Know You Meeting. In this meeting, you need to be as unfettered and specific as possible—as in what would you do if there were no obstacles in front of you? It's funny because we've noticed these meetings start to follow a predictable pattern. People understandably put up an emotional wall. They wonder when we're going to start asking them what's in their wallet. Half an hour into the conversation, the wall starts to come down when they realize we really do care about their lives beyond their wallets. Then it happens. They decide to share that one thing they haven't really shared with many other people. It's usually an idea that if they share, others might think they are crazy. It's the Jumanji drumbeat, that passion within that you cannot stop thinking about. We can sense the weight lifted off their shoulders, and their whole countenance changes.

That's when we lean forward because we can tell we are really getting down to the stuff that matters, the stuff they really want but aren't sure how to pursue.

When we gain that trust and have that level of information, we can help you organize and prioritize your goals and dreams. Invariably, when you consider making a dramatic or even subtle shift in how you do things, there will be obstacles standing in the way of this new path. Most of those obstacles come down to mindset. For example, let's say you are nervous about making a career change. The benefits picture isn't clear on the other side, so you wonder what will happen if you or a family member run into a health-related challenge. What we would do is walk you through pricing options for insurance. What is your out-of-pocket max? How much do you have in savings? With information in hand, paralyzing fear gives way to understanding options and a way forward. When you quantify your fears or challenges and see the numbers right in front of you, it creates a clear decision point. As Bryan always says, numbers don't lie.

Beyond Financial Guilt

This stage of the process is also about helping you get beyond some of the stumbling blocks people experience around money. The process can be painful and challenging for some people. When you are at a low point financially or emotionally, it can be difficult to dream, much less share those dreams with others.

When it comes down to it, most of us experience guilt or regret about where we are financially. We don't measure up to what others have and where we think we ought to be. This also happens to people who make less than they thought they would be making or those making a lot of money each month, but spending more on debt. From people working two jobs to make ends meet to high-earning doctors, we all are susceptible to these thoughts and perspectives.

But there is so much in life that is uncertain. Sometimes events happen that are beyond our control, like an illness or an accident.

Sometimes we just make the wrong decision and take a hit financially. Life happens, and when you are having financial difficulties, it's easy to feel guilty about that.

Financial shame is one of the biggest reasons people cite for why they don't want to sit down with a financial advisor.

Think about your current financial situation. Do you wish you were in a different spot? You are not alone. Yet instead of seeking out advice, many people just suffer in silence.

We want to take shame out of the equation. Ups and downs happen for everyone. If you didn't grow up in a family that taught basic financial literacy, those are just the cards you've been dealt. The bottom line is we have seen business owners, doctors, and lawyers having these thoughts and feelings too. It is time to work through that guilt and start a new path for your future.

Part of this process is examining where the guilt is coming from. Are you looking at other people who seem to have more "things" than you do? Have you made bad investment decisions? Have you seen the people closest to you making "better" decisions than you have? Are you living outside your means and have no idea that you are? When you first start working and making money, the idea that you can afford things can be alluring. You sign up for that store credit card or buy things you have wanted for a while because you think to yourself, "I can afford that monthly payment." What we fail to realize is that those payments add up, and the things we are purchasing are not assets.

There are so many reasons why someone would be hesitant to talk about their current financial situation. Whatever the reason, financial guilt is real. Money is a necessary part of life, but it shouldn't be something that keeps you up at night. The Uncommon Process is meant to help you get out of that vicious cycle of guilt.

Whenever there is guilt about something in your life, there is healing in talking about it and exposing it. Talking to people you trust is powerful. Even if the other person just listens, it is therapeutic to address your concerns and worries. This could be with a counselor, a spouse, or a close friend. Whoever you decide to confide in, you will find that confession is the first step to a new you.

There is a story we like to share about bison. During challenging times in life, you've got to think like a bison. When a storm is on the horizon, bison don't run away from it, they start walking toward it. Crazy, right? But here's the cool part: ultimately, a bison gets through the storm much faster because it walks through it. Other animals walk away from the storm and end up being caught up in it much longer because they didn't confront it head-on.

When life hands you challenging times, don't be so quick to run away and try to hide from the problems. Face them head on, and you will likely get through them much faster. Your biggest failures are sometimes the most important lessons you will ever learn. Failure is a part of life. If you aren't failing, are you really trying?

We have never met anyone who wasn't grateful to acknowledge their financial worries, get the feelings of guilt off their chest, and create a plan to move forward.

It's a new day, so let's make a plan!

The Uncommon Path

Whether you are coming to the process with burdens about how you have managed money in the past or just uncertainty about what to do next, building your Uncommon Life takes some planning. Here is a step-by-step measure of how we help clients do this.

We love helping people galvanize their Uncommon Path. This path is about doing the things God has gifted them to do, and ultimately achieving the time and money freedom to pursue that path, wherever it takes them.

After working together with our clients for nearly a decade, sharing in their hopes and dreams, we've learned a few things. Here is a quick view of the Uncommon Process. We will be getting into further detail on these in later chapters.

Step 1—You must have a budget

Goal: You need to establish a baseline of where you are and determine the amount of income you need to cover your expenses.

This seems like a basic step, but so many of the people we meet are just flying by the seat of their pants in terms of their family finances. Crossing your fingers after hoping that your income will cover your basic monthly expenses is okay if you are not trying to build your wealth, but to really set yourself up for success, you need to know your numbers.

This is a basic and essential starting point to Uncommon Wealth. If you don't have a clear handle on your numbers, you cannot scale your dollars into financial independence.

One question we ask clients is, "If you don't have a clear sense of the day-to-day and what you need to live on, how will you ever know when you are financially free?" In the next chapter, we will get into some specific budgeting tools, but just understand that Step 1 is knowing your numbers.

Step 2—Building a Capital Fund

Goal: To save three to twelve months of living expenses. The duration depends on your risk tolerance and how aggressively you want to approach the investment phase.

Once you have a budget established, you know how much is coming in and how much is going out. If you don't have a surplus each month, it may be time to get nasty and motivated to cut your spending. If you have a surplus, it's now time to put a savings cushion in place in the form of an emergency fund or capital fund.

Here's a scenario for building your emergency fund. Let's say you spend $7,000 a month and you bring in $10,000 a month in household income. That's $3,000 a month toward your capital fund.

Our rule of thumb is to have a six-month reserve easily accessible to meet your basic obligations. So, in this scenario, a six-month emergency fund would equal $42,000 in cash. If you are saving $3,000 a month, then it should take you 14 months to save $42,000. Also, when you have multiple sources of income, you're less likely to use your emergency fund because the probably of losing multiple sources at one time is low.

It is our belief that in the absence of vision, you should pay off your debt. By vision we mean a way that you could invest in something you are passionate about and understand to yield a higher return and more money through one of the Seven Sources of Residual Income.

Which brings us to Step 3.

Step 3—Making Sound Investments

Goal: To do something you are passionate about that eventually builds up the assets and/or cash-flow that replace your monthly living expenses.

Now that you have a budget locked down and a capital fund built up, it's time to look at investing. Our framework for looking at and evaluating investments is the Seven Sources of Residual Income. Investments are personal and can take many forms. It's not just about stocks and bonds. It is about tailoring these options to the individual based on their passions, skills, and expertise.

The Seven Sources of Residual Income:

1. Uncommon Banking—earning a return on savings
2. Real Estate
3. Investments
4. Business
5. Subscription Model/Affiliate Income
6. Intellectual Property
7. Network Marketing

The first source of residual income has historically been earning a return or yield on your savings or emergency fund. In the current low-interest-rate environment, that source has been greatly diminished. Our solution to this is helping individuals and families, through Uncommon Banking, leverage cash-value life insurance to create an alternate banking system. You have access to an ever-increasing pool of cash, a return on that pool in the form of dividends, plus tax protection. This method of saving provides you with a resource to draw from when an opportunity comes along for a sound investment.

An investment strategy needs to be tailored to your goals, your gifts, and your season in life in order to take advantage of opportunities beyond mutual funds and stocks. Sources two through seven are considered investments because they carry risk and the loss of your investment. Remember that our goal is not to get our clients to focus on all seven sources, but to focus on the wealth path that gets them most excited and in line with their passions, gifts, and dreams.

Step 4—Time Freedom

Goal: You are living out your Legacy Vision now, refining your investments with the wisdom and knowledge you have gained in covering your monthly expenses and mentoring others in the path you paved.

Time freedom, or what most people call "retirement," means reaching the point where your monthly expenses are covered by your residual income. Now you have the tools to answer that earlier question, "How will you ever know when you are financially free?"

Does this mean a life of complete leisure? For some, it might. But most of the time, when people love what they do, there's no need to stop. Warren Buffet doesn't have to work, but he loves what he does.

Time freedom does mean you can set your own schedule. It means your business concerns can function without you there every day, and you know your financial bases are covered now and into the future.

It's exciting when we learn about people's hopes and dreams and begin to set up a plan for how they can move forward with those dreams. It's what we love about what we do. Yep, that's right, it matches our passions, our gifts, and our dreams. We are right there with you on our own Uncommon Path.

A Glimpse Down the Uncommon Path:

Kevin Bourke & Patty Neubauer – A Free Eight-Plex

Owning one rental unit can help your cash flow. Two is better. The more you rent, the more money you have flowing through your economic engine. But there are challenges too. Buying an eight-plex rather than six to eight separate units creates economies of scale that are hard to ignore.

That's what happened with Kevin Bourke. As a coach for Iowa State University in Ames, he was looking for some side income to augment his coaching salary. Coaching track in the '80s and '90s was not a huge money-maker. He told us that he and his wife, Patty, wanted to retire at some point. They thought real estate might put them in a position to get there more quickly.

Kevin was buying properties all over Ames. He bought a duplex, and another property he converted into a tri-plex. As his inventory grew, it turned into a lot of running around. It was working financially, but Kevin was working pretty hard to manage and maintain those properties all over the city.

Kevin had an idea to sell his properties. For some entrepreneurs, it's hard to know when to sell, but Kevin sold all of his properties and built an eight-plex. That seemed to be a big answer to the running around question. It was a little bit scary to make the move into this larger asset, compared with the pretty standard home purchases he had been making.

But he found that consolidation in this way made so much sense. It was working well. After selling the other properties, he could focus his time and energy in one place but still have the cash flow from eight units. The Monopoly board game comes to mind where you wipe away the four green homes on your tiles to put down the bigger, shinier red hotel.

One eight-plex is great, but the most interesting part of Kevin's story is what happened next. A property near the eight-plex came on the market. With the equity he had in the first, Kevin found he didn't even need to put any additional money down in order to purchase the second eight-plex.

He told us, "It was actually nerve-racking, believe it or not, buying another building and not having to pay a dime." But of course, he did it, and has not looked back.

Here's one of the big lessons of this approach: when you look at building wealth in our cyclical economy, people who have a lot of money are buying and selling things, then taking gains and consolidating those gains into other, bigger assets.

When he is not managing his properties, Kevin Bourke serves as the President and CEO of the Ames Convention & Visitors Bureau. Prior to this, he spent years as a track and field coach at Iowa State University and the COO at the Iowa Sports Foundation. If you want to hear more about their story, check out the podcast at: **https://www.uncommonwealth.com/podcasts/kevin-bourke**

Uncommon Wealth Tactics:

Often, we meet people who know their budget and what they make, and there isn't much left over. In personal finance, there is a lot of emphasis on cutting your spending and living below what you make. Those are good principles because in life, once we achieve a standard of living, it is hard to give up.

With that said, we feel like equal or greater emphasis needs to be put on increasing your income and the sources with which you make it. In the Current section we want you to list out your current sources of income. This includes all sources of income. If you are making $50 a month extra teaching piano, we want you to list it. In the Future section, we want you list out the other ways you have dreamed of making money as you read the analogy of the Bricklayers and the rest of Chapter 4: Where You Are Now and Where You Want to Be.

◈ Income Sources

Current	Future
1.)	1.)
2.)	2.)
3.)	3.)
4.)	4.)

Here is an example:

◈ Income Sources

Current	Future
1.) Ben's Wage	1.) Ben's LLC
2.) Susan's Wage	2.) Ben's Social Security
3.) Ben's LLC	3.) Susan's Social Security
4.)	4.) Building Rent from LLC

CHAPTER 6

Budgeting: You Need to Know Your Monthly Expenses

Two of the most important questions in financial planning or retirement income planning are:

1. "What do you spend a month?"

2. "When are you going to pass away or 'graduate' (as we call it)?"

It is always amazing to us how many people don't know the answer to the first question. Here's the thing: if you truly want to go down this Uncommon Path, it must start with budgeting. You have to know what you need on a monthly basis to cover your expenses. What's your monthly "nut"?

If you don't have the answer to that, you aren't ready to go down this path. The good news is, these are the numbers that you deal with every month. There is no reason you can't get a handle on your budget and then head down the Uncommon Path.

Who doesn't want to start doing something they love doing right now? The challenge is that most of us aren't taught how to do that. We are taught to choose a lane, get a job, and plod away working for someone else. But of course, the process of understanding our gifts, talents, and passions takes time and looks different for everyone.

We are pushed to get a job to pay our bills, but many of us are never challenged or taught to make money in what we are good at and how to maximize our God-given gifts. Uncommon Wealth is all about helping people start investing in themselves and their skills, dreams, and experiences.

We recently met with a woman who hates her job—really, really hates it. In our meeting with her, she went on about how she couldn't work in the environment at her office anymore. She had an idea for a business she wanted to start but didn't know how to move forward. We have these conversations frequently with clients. We asked, "Do you want to know the most important next step?" She did. We told her she has to know her monthly budget—how much she needs a month to cover her expenses.

It is crucial to know how much income is coming in and what expenses are going out, so we know how much income needs to be replaced. She wasn't sure and didn't seem ready to figure it out. We told her as politely as possible that she would likely be working at that job she hates until she's willing to get real about her monthly numbers.

You have to be ready to do the work on this path because we cannot and will not do it for you. If you really want to start a business, the responsibility is yours. She wants one thing: she can't stand to live her current reality another day, but she is not willing to do the next step to change her course. So does she really want it?

Imagine being trapped in a deep, dark jail cell. You are crying out for help. Is anyone there? You hear a voice saying, "Yes, I am here, and I know how to help you. If you get up and find your way to the door, the key is in the door. You just have to turn it and let yourself out." This woman basically told us she wants to stay in prison. That is something we hate to see.

Why do we belabor this point? Because so many times when we meet with people, they know what they need to do, but are too scared or stuck to take the steps that need to be taken. So they are immobilized and take no action. The status quo is what they know, so they don't want to mess with it.

But here's the thing: regardless of whether you take one path or the other, understanding your budget is incredibly important. Without understanding the bottom line, it's hard to dream big. Wouldn't you rather know that you can pay your bills and completely love your life than make more money that is keeping you trapped where you don't want to be?

We've found that most who take the Uncommon Path don't regret it. This doesn't mean that your bank account is going to skyrocket right away. Your mindset changes from one of being a victim, of living with regrets, of feeling chained up, to one of freedom, expression, purpose, and embracing the uncomfortable.

The numbers don't lie, but that can be a good thing. Often people fear things because they seem big or financially out of reach. When we help people look at the numbers and take emotion out of the equation, they quickly realize that the big, scary monster isn't so scary after all. But it all starts with a budget. It all starts with knowing what is coming in and what is going out on a monthly basis.

Is this fun, exactly? No. Nobody wants to do it, but when you change your mindset to the end goal, the task becomes bearable. Think of it this way:

A budget is the key to unlocking my money, which can be used as a tool to help me design the life I want to live.

Budgeting with a vision of the life you dream about reminds

you that money is a tool. You then use that tool to unlock your God-given gifts and talents to live an Uncommon Life. The challenge most people have is in monetizing those ideas and replacing their paycheck. We will get to that in the investment chapter coming up, but for now you need a budget to get there. In later chapters, we are going to look in depth at a concept called the 4% rule of retirement income. We will show you how it can give you an estimate of what you need to be financially free. Quickly, the 4% rule means for every $100 a month you need, you will need $30,000 in assets to cover that expense.

Uncommon Budgeting

What if you could understand and unlock your cash flow in less than 90 days? That's what can happen with the Uncommon Budgeting Process.

Understanding your monthly "nut"—the dollar amount you need in order to pay all your obligations—is the starting point to getting your cash flow moving in the right direction.

That's why having a budget that keeps track of your Now Money is so important. If your obligations like mortgage, car payment, utilities, etc. add up to $7,000 a month and your household income is $10,000 a month, you've got to know where the rest of that $3,000 is going. So many people at every income level live paycheck to paycheck because they don't have a budget. When you just spend without having a budget in mind, that $3,000 gap between your income and monthly obligations closes before you know it. Without a budget that includes discretionary spending, your money goes into that black hole of venti cappuccinos and Amazon purchases.

A word to those who have little or nothing left over each month, or end each month in the red: this Uncommon Path is even more important for you in our opinion. So many people have repeatedly cut their expenses, and don't see anything left to cut. You can only cut so much before you give up on your dreams and lose interest. Pushing your budget that hard and putting some of that money away in an IRA—which feels like some vague, distant future—isn't going to help you psychologically or emotionally. Remember our first bricklayer? His level of candor with his day job may be in response to this type of behavior, lifestyle, and lack of results. What you and our bricklayer really need is to increase your income.

"No kidding, Sherlock!" (or something a little less kind) might be what you're thinking. But bear with us in this budgeting process, and we'll reward you with Chapters 8, 9, and 10, which are *all about* creative ways to generate residual income. But to prepare for those chapters and investing in things that increase your income, you need the foundation we build in the next two chapters on not only building a budget, but building a capital account.

These principles around budgeting are crucial as you scale your life and aim for time freedom.

Big companies like Amazon track their money. They operate with clear budgeting guidelines. Having clear guidelines in your household will ultimately help you increase your cash flow, build your wealth, and give you that time freedom.

Banking Structure

Before we jump into budgeting tactics, we want to take a moment to talk about how we organize our bank accounts. We meet with lots of folks, and what follows is pretty much every person's structure for banking and spending. You have a checking account where your paychecks are deposited, and you have a savings account for the emergency money. Sound familiar? We see major problems with this for most people who don't have a budget because it's a confusing setup.

Most people get paid bi-weekly or sometimes even weekly. Every week, you have new money coming into your account. And every day you have money going out through bills on auto pay, checks written out, big box store and main street shopping, and those late night purchases online. Well, if you set a monthly budget and everything is happening through that one checking account, it's chaos. Most people cannot track day-to-day where things stand relative to their budget.

We advocate for families to create two separate bank accounts for simplicity. Families then have an "IN" checking account and an "OUT" checking account. They set up a new joint checking account for the "IN" account because it is easier to change your direct deposit at work to a different account. All paychecks and any money they receive goes into that account. The old checking account is now the "OUT" account where expenses are paid and the debit cards you are used to spending from are tied. It is much more difficult to change all of your spending habits versus changing a couple of paychecks. They can do this with no overdraft repercussions by making each account the other's overdraft protection.

This structure helps separate what is happening within each account throughout the month, and it is very easy to see at a high level where you are at in your budget. Now that we have that laid out, let's dig into the actual budgeting process.

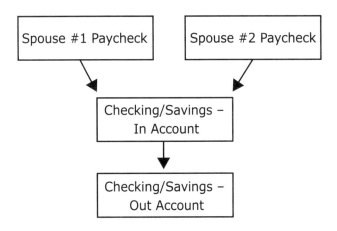

Building Your Budget

Of course, the idea of having a budget is not Uncommon, but the practices of creating and sticking to a budget are far too Uncommon. We want to help you fix that if you have not committed to a budgeting process. If you have a budgeting system that works for you, and you are consistently tracking your numbers, then kudos to you. Keep working that system.

When it comes to budgeting, there are apps for that. To create a budget, you can go to many platforms, follow many different tricks, tweaks, systems, and ideas. These can be helpful, but in life is there really a substitute for hard work and getting your hands dirty? Doing the work of budgeting will make income and expenses more tangible, so you can really understand where you are starting from in building your Uncommon Life. It is work, but it does not have to be compli-cated. Budgeting can be overwhelming, so we want to boil it down to its simplest form. Here is our four-step process to creating and sticking to a budget.

WORDS OF WISDOM: If you seriously want to put a budget together or improve what you are doing, we encourage you to read the next section to understand the process, then intentionally schedule time to come back and really work through this process to establish a budget. As we have said before, this is hard. This isn't fun for a lot of people, and this is going to take some real time to complete. Please do something and start somewhere.

Step 1—90 Days of Data

The first step of our budgeting process is printing off the last 90 days (three months) of statements from the accounts you are spending out of. For example, bank statements, credit card statements, and/or your payroll stub if you are direct-depositing part of your salary to other accounts. In our view, just printing them off and getting them in your hands is the best way because it forces you to dig in and do the work. Now that you have those statements in front of you, we are going to walk through the next step.

Step 2—What Did You Spend

Now that you have everything in front of you the goal of step two is to calculate what you truly spent over the last 90 days and figure out a monthly average. Add up all the transactions that were expenditures from your accounts. We want to tally the money that went out.

Your bank statements and credit card statements should tell you what the activity summary was for the month, so you can use that if you want, but we recommend actually adding up all the transactions quickly. This forces you to look at everything you spent money on.

We are not asking you to categorize your expenses or make 100 envelopes, but the practice of going through and adding up your expenses starts to make your mind and your conscience more aware of where your money is going.

Calculate the monthly totals for the last 90 days. This will give you three months' worth of transactions, which is a pretty good indicator of your monthly spending. Now, add up the three monthly spending totals and divide by three. That is your monthly average.

Now do the same thing for your income. It's important to start to realize how much is really coming into your bank account and how much is really going out. The goal of this awareness is mindfulness. If you want to get ahead financially, you need to start dictating what your money is doing. Add up each of the monthly totals and divide by three again to obtain your monthly average income.

Now, subtract your expenses for each month from your income. Add those three numbers up and divide by three. That is the monthly average of what you have left over (hopefully), or what you are over-spending on average.

Step 3—Start Tracking for the Next 90 Days

Now that you have 90 days in the rear-view mirror, it is time to start doing this exercise at the end of the next three months. You will be adding up your expenses and your income for the month and determining what is left over or how much you came up short. Compare that to the last three months' totals and averages to see where you are. Many of our clients report they are spending nearly 10% less a month just from this work.

This budgeting process is simple, and it is easier to make minor adjustments. There are no categories, envelopes, or large sums of cash being taken out. This is simple stuff. The last thing we want is for you to be lost in the budgeting portion of finances. And we know that in marriages, this is where many fights can be started. Simplicity is most often best. At the end of six months, you now have half a year's spending habits in hand. You have probably learned a lot about yourself and made some meaningful changes to your spending habits without any really complicated process or tracking.

This is where we move past monthly budgeting and want you to focus now on building a surplus of cash that we call a "Capital Fund." If you want to go deeper into the budget and use categories, envelopes, and tracking apps, you can, but a mentor once told us this and we have never forgotten it: a lot of people spend too much time tracking budgets and pinching pennies to save a few bucks when they should be more focused on doubling their income.

If you are reading this book, it is probably not to get lost in a budgeting process that takes hours and hours. It is to find new ways to make money and to have your money working while you sleep, so let's keep going.

Budgeting may seem deadly boring, but *you can do this*!

We don't want to lose you here. You have all the information you need. In order to make changes or chart a new course, you must know these numbers. You have to know the income that you need to replace with residual income.

And if you already have a system and know your numbers, that is fantastic. No need to reinvent the wheel, just work with the budget numbers you have firmly in your grasp.

What is the net result?

The whole point here is not only knowing your monthly "nut," but also being brutally honest with yourself. Are you spending more than you are making? If you are, starting a business or quitting a job is a horrible idea and a recipe for disaster. If you are consistently bringing in more than you spend, great job. If your number is negative, let's figure out how to change that. Chapter 7 will be a great place to start.

A Glimpse Down the Uncommon Path:

Scott and Joanna Larsen – It's Paid Off

When we first met with Scott and Joanna, their life and finances were not out of line at all. They did desire some direction and wanted our feedback to help create a plan moving forward. They were open, talking a lot about what they wanted, but resoundingly didn't have that thing that they knew they wanted to capitalize on. Scott had a good job, was interested in the idea of being financially independent and retiring early, but didn't have an idea of how he wanted to generate extra income. Our motto is, "In the absence of vision, pay off debt," so we started to talk about paying off his primary mortgage.

As we explored all the ideas of paying off their debt, Bryan built two models. The first included a seven-year plan that accounted for vacations, home projects, etc. The second was a four-and-a-half-year plan to pay down faster with "no frills."

The race was on. We helped them set up a financial model that gave them flexibility and control. With their hard work and determination, they paid off their primary mortgage. Scott and Joanna were unified on that target and didn't stop until it was achieved. They stopped contributing above the match to his retirement account at work to free up some additional cash flow. After understanding the risks and rewards, we decided to switch his mortgage from a 15-year fixed to a Home Equity Line of Credit (HELOC), so that the mortgage instrument was less amortized and more liquid if he needed to get the money back they were overpaying on the house.

Their journey was quicker than we all thought. Though they were met with some turbulence, after regrouping and taking a few months off in the middle to grab a dog and go on a vacation, it was back to shredding that debt. And then it happened. By month 29, they hit their goal. The house was paid off. Quite a bit shorter than four and a half years. With a clear focus and unified goal, it's amazing what you can achieve.

Uncommon Wealth Tactics:

List out your liabilities and put them in your Uncommon Financial Dashboard. List them all out, from Mortgages to Credit Cards and Student Loans. If you owe someone money, write them down in the Current Debts Section. Even medical bills.

Current Debts

1.)

2.)

3.)

4.)

Here is an example of what it should look like filled out:

 Current Debts

1.) Mortgage $467,000

2.) Ben's Car $29,000

3.) Susan's Car $22,000

4.) Ben's Student Loan $48,000

The total Debt is $566,000.

Now that you have your liabilities, it is time to move on and learn about your assets in Chapter 7.

CHAPTER 7

Building Your Capital Fund

Taking Inventory to Build a War Chest

It starts with a budget, but it can't end there. With a budget in place, you can begin to get your money working for you, instead of the other way around. Knowing what your monthly expenses are is a great start toward Uncommon Wealth. Too many people know what they earn, get a handle on what they spend in a month, then use the excess to start funding retirement accounts. Because that is what everyone is supposed to do, right? Not if you are trying to build Uncommon Wealth.

We speak to a lot of people about money, and invariably someone asks, "Where should I put my money?" We always say without hesitation, "Put $50,000 in the bank." Why? Because it's hard to do for most people. The mindset that is created from pooling cash creates discipline and proof you can accomplish something big. Not to mention, this money is liquid and accessible. It's not tied up in a retirement account.

In this chapter, our goal is to help you see your assets in a different way, make sure you have that 50,000 or six months' living expenses in the bank, and organize your accounts to support your goals. To do that, we need to create a baseline of where your money is. One of the things frequently overlooked by most advisors and entrepreneurs is the types of money you have.

Two Types of Money—Seeing Your Assets in a Different Way

There are only two types of money. Now Money and Later Money. This is one of the basic concepts we teach in order to help people think beyond a common approach to financial planning. There is Now Money, like a paycheck, and there is Later Money, like an IRA or 401(k). Now Money is there for ready access. Later Money stacked away in retirement accounts can be helpful, but too often, financial planning puts too much focus on that Later Money and not enough on the Now Money.

A big part of what makes us uncommon as wealth advisors is our focus on Now Money—putting your money to work for you before age 65, not after. You have big dreams for the here and now. And here's a point we make again and again with clients: *you* are your greatest asset. We think that investing right now in you and your dreams is the way to gain dividends now and into your bright future.

How do you look at your dreams for the present without stealing from your retirement? Investing in assets that produce cash flow now that can help design your life today, requires Now Money. Those assets can and will also be a powerful tool as you achieve time freedom; they just require a different mindset versus maxing out a retirement plan. People are scared to use their Now Money, but there are so many ways to grow your wealth besides a 401(k) or IRA. There are strategies that help you grow your Now Money so it is not all stockpiled into that bucket you can only access later. In the following chapters, we will dive into different ways to use your Now Money to help finance your present and prepare for the future.

But before that, there is some work to do. It starts with establishing a baseline and decision point to move forward. Where is your money invested? What are you adding to the account monthly (if anything), and what goal is it serving?

Let's look at Now Money versus Later Money and the way different accounts are registered for tax purposes in the traditional sense.

At this point, just like the budgeting session, print off all your statements. If you can't get your statements, call customer service or your advisor and get all your investment and other account statements printed out on the kitchen table.

Now Types of Money

These are accounts or registrations that you have paid tax on that don't have penalties or rules about accessing the money right now.

Checking, Savings, Joint Tenancy with Rights of Survivorship (JTWROS), Individual, Revocable Trust—These are all registrations that you can use to hold money in the bank or invest with after taxes. Think of this like paycheck money you have paid taxes on and can use on anything you want.

Cash-Value Life Insurance—Life insurance for cash value has tax protection similar to a Roth IRA with one major distinction. You can borrow against the cash-value and growth now without waiting until 59-and-a-half and it still can earn dividends on that money like it was still there. There are no government restrictions on how much you can make in order to contribute. And there are no rules on how much you can contribute annually.

Home Equity—This is the equity that you build over time in your primary residence or rental property through down payments, equity accrual as the mortgage is paid, and if your home appreciates in value.

Hybrid Money Registrations

There are a few registrations that act kind of like hybrid registrations for the Uncommon Path. These registrations are more friendly in repositioning funds after we meet to help accelerate your Capital Fund and to build wealth more quickly depending on your goals.

Roth IRA—You have already paid taxes on this money. The principal can be accessed for Now Money. If held for five years, you can take your principal out without penalty.

Health Savings Accounts (HSA)—This is money set aside for health expenses. It's tax-deferred and accessed tax-free, but has a ton of rules on how it can be used and how much you can put into it.

College Savings or Child Focused Investment Accounts—529, Coverdell Education Savings Accounts, Uniform Gifts To Minors Act (UGMA), Uniform Transfers to Minors Act (UTMA), etc.—These are accounts focused on saving for kids for college with some form of tax deduction like 529s, or shifting the social security that reports the growth and earnings like UGMA or UTMA accounts.

Later Types of Money

These are accounts or registrations available without penalty around the age of 59-and-a-half, typically for income after retirement.

401(k), 403(b), 457, Solo 401(k), SIMPLE IRA, SEP-IRA, ESOP, Pension Plan, Traditional IRA, etc.—These are the traditional retirement plan setups that most companies use for their employees. 401(k) is for for-profit corporations. 403(b) is for non-profit organizations like hospitals and schools and 457 accounts are for government employees.

Non-Qualified Annuities—This basically turns the money into Later Money as withdrawals shouldn't be made before 59-and-a-half. Withdrawals prior to 59-and-a-half come with a 10 percent penalty similar to an IRA.

Building Your Capital Fund

This is where things start to get exciting. This is the fork in the road where you need to evaluate, unlearn, and relearn because most financial planning you have been taught is focused almost exclusively on Later Money.

We are looking at what assets you have to work with to help you accomplish your goals. We look at your situation through the lens of a financial planner because that is the industry we are in, and those are the regulations that govern us. Second, we look at your numbers in relation to the goals you have expressed that are important to you.

Most of our clients are at a place in life where they want something different and they need help getting there. If that is just time freedom or retiring, then in large part most of our planning is traditional in the sense of putting together retirement income plans and mitigating the risks associated.

For the rest who aren't 59-and-a-half and are looking to start a side business or want real estate investments or to launch a business before 59-and-a-half, that is where the advice may differ if they are truly serious. As we mentioned, these types of investments require Now Money and a different account registration of where to store your capital. That way you can access those funds to make the investments you desire.

Now you have a budget in place and you are putting money away every month. Simply put, we want you to have six to 12 months of your income or cash flow needs saved up and banked in Now Money for what others would say is an emergency fund. For example, looking at the last chapter and seeing that we are spending on average $8,300 a month, means we should have $49,800 to $99,600 in liquid savings. We look at this more as a Capital Fund.

We call this a Capital Fund for two main reasons. The first is mindset and the second is that it takes money to make money.

You need some cash on hand accessible enough that you can use it when things happen. The downside of holding a lot of money in a savings account is that the bank doesn't owe you anything anymore due to the low interest rates. You are paying a price on liquidity, trapping money that could be doing multiple things at the same time. That is where we segue to our Uncommon roots and show you how to mobilize an emergency or capital fund that works for you.

Savings or capital is the springboard into investing. When you look at buying that first rental property or Airbnb, you need a down payment. You need money in the bank. If you want to launch that business or start investing in the stock market in an after-tax (Now Money) type of account, you need capital and a cushion. One of the leading causes of entrepreneurs failing is a lack of capital.

We have included an amazingly simple worksheet to use for this step that will help you determine if you are investing to support your goals. You can find this worksheet here: **www.uncommon wealth.com/BuildingYourCapitalFund**. The goal of the worksheet is for you to see on one page the two different types of money you have.

Now, with a budget inventory of all your assets, we can move to the fun part: growing and building your net worth through the Seven Sources of Residual Income. Let's go!

A Glimpse Down the Uncommon Path:

The Landlord Dentist

When you have Uncommon dreams, sometimes it's hard to find the right support system. There will always be those who say, "No, you can't do things that way." But there are so many ways to create sources of income for your family. Here's a great story about creating multiple sources of residual income using several different strategies.

When the building our dentist was renting for his dental practice came on the market, he was ready to jump at the chance. Another set of advisors advised him against it, but he is young and hungry and wanted to make it work. He wanted something that could drive another source of income for him and his wife but also become an economic driver in the growing community where they lived and worked.

Like most of us, they aren't made of money, so at first, they thought about going in with several investors to purchase the building. But when they came to meet with us, we showed them how they could make the purchase themselves by cashing out an investment account. We cautioned them about purchasing the building with multiple investors and needing a "committee" of five other people to make decisions.

The dentist agreed. He just had not seen a way forward before. They purchased the building, and it has been a terrific investment. Just like any other venture, it has not been without its challenges. One of the risks in owning investment properties is an obvious one: occupancy rates. Since the purchase, one tenant has left and he is trying to fill that vacancy. But even with that small setback, the purchase has brought other intangibles like depreciation and a sense of ownership and pride in the community.

All this sounds great. He's operating a dental practice and a real estate company. But these businesses require cash. What is a good solution for this? The Landlord Dentist has leveraged Uncommon Banking via cash-value life insurance to help build liquidity, but also to provide death benefit coverage for his family and business as well as further tax protection and compound interest.

The Landlord Dentist also has a retirement plan through his dental practice for him and his employees. When you add all these together, the Landlord Dentist is leveraging their Now Money to build wealth four different ways, all from starting out owning a dental practice. And the fifth way is Later Money through the 401(k) retirement plan which provides him with an employee benefit and a tax deduction for his contributions.

Uncommon Wealth Tactics:

List all your assets, from checking and savings accounts to expensive artwork. If your car has value, you can put that in this number as well. Don't forget the current value of what you could sell your house for today. Remember any 401(k) account and Roth account as well. We will go into more detail about this later, but document your accounts in this area. If you have completed your Building Your Capital Fund document, these should be easy to fill out.

Building Your
Capital Fund

 Now Money	Hybrid Money	Later Money
(Checking, Savings, JTWROS, Individual Accounts, Revocable Trust, Equity in House, and Cash-Value Life Insurance)	*(Roth IRA, Health Savings Accounts (HSA), College Savings or Child Focused Investment Accounts – 529, Coverdell Education Savings Accounts, Uniform Gifts To Minors Act (UGMA), Uniform Transfers to Minors Act (UTMA), etc.*	*401(k), 403(b), 457, Solo 401(k), SIMPLE IRA, SEP IRA, ESOP, Pension Plan, Traditional IRA, Non-Qualified Annuities etc.*
1.	1.	1.
2.	2.	2.
3.	3.	3.
4.	4.	4.
5.	5.	5.
Total	**Total**	**Total**

*Disclaimer Depending on your risk tolerance and tax situation depends if you should cash out any "Later Money". You don't have to liquidate any of these, but know how to access these if you would need them is part of your Capital Fund. Advisory Services are offered through Uncommon Wealth Partners, LLC a registered investment advisor.

 **Currently Wealth Building**

 Real Estate

 Business

Savings

 Retirement

Here is an example of this Section filled out:

Currently Wealth Building

Real Estate $530,000

Business $10,000

Savings $80,000 Bank
$45,000 Life Insurance Cash

Retirement $280,000 Susan's 401k
$255,000 Ben's 401k

Once you have those all down, add them up, and those are your assets. The total of your Assets is $1,200,000. Now let's move on to Chapter 8 and look at potential new ways to increase your income and your assets at the same time.

CHAPTER 8

Investing in the Seven Sources of Residual Income—Uncommon Banking

Well, here we are. We are at the heart of what it means to build wealth beyond those Later Money tools you've been taught about your entire life. There are so many other ways to increase cash flow and build wealth without deferring all your Now Money into those Later Money retirement accounts.

If it's not clear yet, your primary investment should be in yourself. When you invest time, money, and other resources into honing your skills, developing the talents you have, and pursuing what brings you joy, the Return On You (ROY) is unbeatable. When you invest in yourself, you give yourself the tools to pursue all these other avenues for building residual income. You build the confidence to test things out, fail sometimes, and find what works.

The days of choosing a company and spending your entire career working there are near extinction. For most of us, that scenario has gone the way of the dinosaur. But many people still think that work and a retirement plan are the only ways to create income.

And while we love the entrepreneurial spirit, we want you to understand that you don't necessarily need to ditch a job that pays your bills to start generating residual income. Whether you choose the purely entrepreneurial track or stay working for someone else, you should still be thinking of ways to build wealth beyond the everyday working world.

We've identified Seven Sources of Residual Income that are within anyone's reach. We've known friends, family, and clients who dip a toe into one, two, or several of these income opportunities. Let's take a closer look at how these sources of income might help you reach time freedom.

Here's the quick list, followed by a deep dive into each:

- **Uncommon Banking**

- **Real Estate**

- **Investing**

- **Business**

- **Subscription Model and Affiliate Income**

- **Intellectual Property**

- **Network Marketing**

We are in an age where we have so many investment choices, it may seem overwhelming. But understand that your Uncommon Path is your own. It might involve one or two of these sources of income. It might involve more if that's where your gifts and interests are. And you might move in and out of some over time.

The point of understanding these sources of income is to create a path that makes the most of your gifts, talents, and passions. The end goal is time freedom to live life on your own terms.

Okay, with those disclaimers in place, let's take a closer look at the other sources.

SOURCE 1: Uncommon Banking

Why do we keep talking about banking, and how does it fit with residual income? To answer that, we start with saving. Historically speaking, there has been a big emphasis on the wealth impact of saving.

Saving is different from investing. Saving is the expectation of putting money away with little to no risk of losing your money or the principal balance, all while generating a rate of return on that money of 4% to 6%. Looking back on the past 200 years or so, the average rate of interest on savings has been 5% to 6%.

Not these days. In the 21st Century, with national debts spiraling out of control and interest rates being suppressed, for most of the years from 2000 on, we've experienced an environment where low interest, well below 5%, is paid on savings.

Now, let's look at the concept of banking. In life, we save money, and we spend money. Each month, money comes in and money goes out. Guess what? That is banking. Banking is the movement of money through your economic life. This movement of money will happen until you "graduate." Money will come in, and money will go out.

A System That Benefits You

To be successful in business or really anything in life, automation and systems are extremely powerful. For years, we all relied on a system of savings that brought in a return around 5%. With that system broken, what kind of system can you set up that will benefit you? Those checking and savings accounts just do not function that way anymore.

So how do you set up a system that helps you win over time—

a system that truly puts time and interest on your side instead of the banks'? We call that system Uncommon Banking.

We are super passionate about Uncommon Banking because it is a scalable system that leverages a simple economic law and tips the scales of savings and interest in your favor. So how does it work?

Money has a cost. More simply put, money doesn't grow on trees. When people invest money or lend money, they expect a return. They expect to be paid for the use and control of their money. That's why, as small as the return might be at this point in history, we expect to get paid a rate of interest at the bank for leaving our money there. Why? Because the banks get to use our money to lend against, so for that benefit, they should pay us interest on our money.

We save and invest our money to earn an expected return, or else we spend our money and forgo that ability to earn interest. Let's say you have $50 in your wallet. You can invest that money or stop by your favorite burger joint with the family. You order a round of burgers and milkshakes and spend it. When you spend, that $50 is gone from your economic engine and cannot earn interest for you anymore. For a short while, that $50 was a part of your economic system but was then shifted to the burger joint's economic system.

Let's look at this another way: the purchase of a car. We are told by Dave Ramsey (among others) that paying cash is so much better than using debt. There are two main ways that most Americans purchase their vehicles: Cash or Credit (aka: debt).

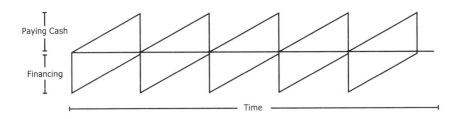

Take a look at the chart on the prior page. When we save up cash to buy a car, we must save over several years to build up enough cash, then we spend it down (that's the straight line to the middle). We save up, then buy, save up, then buy. You can see when we save and buy five vehicles, we are right back where we started.

But lots of people finance their car purchase through an auto loan. Looking at the financing line, it's just the mirror image of paying cash. We take out a loan immediately to buy a car and then we slowly pay it back trying to get the loan paid off. Then, about when the loan is paid off, that car has outlived its usefulness, or we are just ready for something different. But, as you can see, we end up right back where we started.

What if There Was Another Way?

Everything we learn in finance is really designed to separate you from your money. But the rich think about things differently. The rest of us must consciously think about saving and investing. So many of our financial decisions are done in a silo, but the wealthy think about things more holistically. The rest of us have been taught to put into savings for an emergency fund, get a term insurance policy, and give money to the lender to finance our vehicles. It ends up being a lot of money. What if there was a way to earn interest on more of the money that passed through your hands?

Let's look at a typical American monthly budget. For many, including us, our faith calls us to a 10% tithe to the church. Conventional financial planning says you should save 10% in a retirement account (Later Money) for the future. The average two-income family in the U.S. pays about 22% of their income between state, federal, payroll, property, sales, and other taxes. Then another 30% to 40% goes to a mortgage, car, student loan, and credit cards as debt service. The rest is left over for your other discretionary spending: food, utilities, clothes, entertainment, travel, etc. You are tapped out.

This is why the statistics show most Americans are in debt and have little saved. What if we could create a system to combine these cash flows and build another asset along the way? We call this Uncommon Banking.

Common Vs. Uncommon Banking

Let's look at a traditional banking model and why this works the way it does.

A bank pools its money up in a General Fund and then manages deposits and loans.

Which one is the asset for the bank? Which one is the liability for the bank? The bank is paying 1% on the deposits you have with them. They are charging you 5% on the loans you take out with them. So the deposits are the liability and the loans are the asset.

What is the rate of the return for the bank? Well, they are

getting five on the loan minus the one they are giving you on your deposits. $5 - 1 = 4$, but to be clear, that's not just 4%. What the bank gets is four divided by the cost to the bank (which is .01, or 1%) which is 400%!

Current Banking System

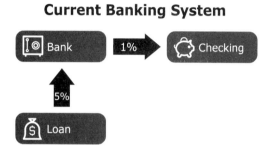

Here is a good way to illustrate this. If you had $1 in a savings account earning 1%, the bank would owe you $.01. Conversely, if you had $1 loaned from the bank at 5%, you would owe the bank $.05. Does the bank have 4% more pennies than you or four times more pennies? Four times is right!

What if there was a different way? We are advocating that there is, and this is how it works.

Uncommon Banking Model

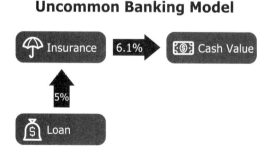

Insurance companies don't necessarily market this way, but when you look at the illustration above, a whole life policy can function very similarly to a bank. But it puts you in the position of the banker. The whole life company pools their cash up like the bank does and then loans it out to generate return for their policy holders and the company itself. For every dollar in guarantees the insurance company has, they must leave a dollar in reserve.

There is another box in the insurance model not shown, which is premium. If you stop paying your premium, the risk goes away for the insurance company, therefore making it a safer model to bank with.

At the time of writing this book, a whole life company is paying 6.1% on the cash value of the policy gross before cost of insurance expenses. They are charging 5% if you take out a loan.

But here is the great thing: when you take out a loan from the whole life company, you are taking it from their general fund. They leave your cash value on deposit, all of it earning dividends.

Giving Your Money Goals a Big Boost with Uncommon Banking

Let's look at three typical money goals for an average American. You want to sock something away in savings every month. You'd like to have some life insurance to cover the unexpected. And you need a car to get around, so you'll probably be making car payments.

Let's say you've been doing well with savings. You've got a $25,000 emergency fund accumulated in a savings account. Way to go!

So your financial life looks a little something like this:

Savings	Term Insurance	Car Payment	Emergency Fund
$500/month	$70/month	$400/month	$25,000

In terms of many people's expectations for wealth-building, this looks like a win. And in many ways, it is. Having $25,000 saved up is a great step. Keeping that momentum going with $500 a month in savings is great. But then there is the other side of the ledger. A $70 insurance payment and $400 a month for a car the family really needs. Poof. That money's gone.

How much of this money is building wealth for you? The $500 a month in savings is building wealth and earning interest, but the interest rate is low, and that money is taxable. Yet this is a path that many people take.

There is a different path you could turn to. What if that $500 a month in savings could earn interest? Think about that from ages 30 to 60. Thirty years times $6,000 is $180,000 of savings with no interest earned. What if that earned a modest interest rate of, say, 4%? At a simple compounding interest rate, and assuming this 4% didn't have a tax liability charged annually, that adds up to $343,756.98. At the time of this writing, rates paid on savings are incredibly low to almost non-existent, ranging from 0% to 2%. Looking at this based on a 2% interest rate would result in $246,037.42. However, adding an additional 2% more interest over 30 years translates into almost another $100,000 of savings.

But wait, there's more. You still have that $25,000 emergency fund that you started this exercise with. Add that in at the start, and now you have $424,841.92.

Think about that for a second. That monthly "money in and money out" in your cash flow could translate into $424,841 by the time you are 60 years old. This is not just money you are socking away and forgetting about. You are using this money (in this scenario) for three things: savings, death benefits, and a decent car.

If that was true, is that something you would want to understand and incorporate into your financial plan?

That is Uncommon Banking.

Here's the beauty of Uncommon Banking: instead of saving money in one place and then tossing money at insurance in another place and a car payment in another, you are putting three cash flows in one place that produces compounding, tax-deferred, and liquid cash value.

Take the money you were putting into savings ($500), along with the term life policy premium ($70), and put that into a whole life insurance premium. Over the next four years, take $5,000 from the emergency fund to overfund your insurance policy. You can do something called "overfunding" on a whole life policy by putting additional funds in a Paid Up Additions rider (PUA). In total you are now putting in $11,840 for the first four years of the policy.

You still need a car, so go ahead and purchase a car every five years. You borrow that against the cash value of your insurance policy, and in effect, you are paying yourself back $400 a month, or $4,800 a year, instead of paying the bank. That plus the on-going $6,840 for the premium adds up to a total annual contribution to the policy of $11,640. If you notice, we haven't changed the cash-flow of our example client at all. We have just repositioned it. Our feeling is that the policy as it pools up cash value acts as that emergency/capital fund for you, putting that money on deposit in your own personal banking system.

If you are paying back your whole life policy loan at $400 per month, you are freeing up some of the lien on your money. The loan amount goes down dollar for dollar. At the end of the year, there will be interest that goes to the insurance company, but our goal is to get that debt paid as fast as possible.

When you use your policy this way and pay a loan off to the insurance company, you are doing two things. First, you are giving yourself access to more money. Second, you are reducing your debt. Over time, the cash value will continue to increase, and the insurance company will owe you more dividends. That loan is just a prepayment on the death benefit.

The results are staggering. You have your life insurance, with an increasing death benefit compared with a 30-year term policy. You get the cars you need. And you have a pile of liquid, tax-free cash that you can access via policy loans. You do not pay tax by accessing your cash-value growth if you take a policy loan. This means you can access the growth of your money without paying tax.

So that $400,000-plus is not just a pot of gold at the end of the rainbow. That money has been working for you this whole time. It's been accumulating via compound interest, and you've been using it to buy those cars. And you can use it to borrow to purchase anything. It is *way* more than a death benefit. The following examples show the potential premiums, dividends, cash value, and death benefits for a typical whole life policy modeled at current dividend rates.

Hypothetical & Non-Guaranteed Values

Year	Age	Total Premium	Dividend	Premium Outlay	Cum. Premium Outlay	Income	Total Loan Balance	Total Net Cash Value	Change in Total Net Cash Value	Change in Net CV Less Prem. Outlay	Total Net Death Benefit w/out Div	Total Net Death Benefit
1	31	11,840	105	11,840	11,840	0	0	6,703	6,703	-5,137	1,382,853	1,382,959
2	32	11,840	233	11,840	23,680	0	0	14,136	7,433	-4,407	1,414,687	1,414,920
3	33	11,840	798	11,840	35,520	0	0	23,082	8,947	-2,893	1,445,966	1,446,764
4	34	11,840	1,018	11,840	47,360	21,983	23,082	12,198	-10,884	-22,724	1,453,650	1,454,668
5	35	6,840	1,349	11,640	59,000	0	18,042	25,897	13,699	2,059	1,458,690	1,460,039
6	36	6,840	1,680	11,640	70,640	0	13,002	39,283	13,386	1,746	1,464,399	1,466,079
7	37	6,840	2,035	11,640	82,280	0	7,962	53,199	13,916	2,276	1,470,760	1,472,796
8	38	6,840	2,387	11,640	93,920	0	2,922	67,690	14,491	2,851	1,477,754	1,480,140
9	39	6,840	2,356	11,640	105,560	22,000	20,982	59,291	-8,399	-20,039	1,462,239	1,464,595
10	40	6,840	2,661	11,640	117,200	0	15,942	74,642	15,351	3,711	1,468,470	1,471,131
11	41	6,840	3,059	11,640	128,840	0	10,902	90,580	15,938	4,298	1,475,219	1,478,278
12	42	6,840	3,405	11,640	140,480	0	5,862	107,225	16,645	5,005	1,482,791	1,486,195
13	43	6,840	3,781	11,640	152,120	0	822	124,604	17,380	5,740	1,490,732	1,494,513
14	44	6,840	3,894	11,640	163,760	22,000	18,882	119,397	-5,207	-16,847	1,475,935	1,479,829
15	45	6,840	4,288	11,640	175,400	0	13,842	138,113	18,715	7,075	1,483,554	1,487,842
16	46	6,840	4,643	11,640	187,040	0	8,802	157,174	19,061	7,421	1,491,515	1,496,157
17	47	6,840	5,032	11,640	198,680	0	3,762	177,109	19,935	8,295	1,499,778	1,504,810
18	48	6,840	5,443	10,423	209,103	0	0	196,708	19,599	9,176	1,507,064	1,512,507
19	49	6,840	5,646	11,640	220,743	22,000	18,060	195,243	-1,465	-13,105	1,492,781	1,498,427
20	50	6,840	6,117	11,640	232,383	0	13,020	217,922	22,679	11,039	1,501,030	1,507,147
21	51	6,840	6,583	11,640	244,023	0	7,980	241,658	23,737	12,097	1,509,574	1,516,158
22	52	6,840	7,071	11,640	255,663	0	2,940	266,446	24,787	13,147	1,518,397	1,525,468
23	53	6,840	7,590	9,640	265,303	0	0	290,223	23,778	14,138	1,525,368	1,532,958
24	54	6,840	7,932	11,640	276,943	22,000	18,060	293,905	3,682	-7,958	1,511,532	1,519,464
25	55	6,840	8,532	11,640	288,583	0	13,020	321,896	27,991	16,351	1,520,332	1,528,863
26	56	6,840	9,175	11,640	300,223	0	7,980	351,195	29,299	17,659	1,529,394	1,538,569
27	57	6,840	9,820	11,640	311,863	0	2,940	381,889	30,694	19,054	1,538,720	1,548,540
28	58	6,840	10,465	9,640	321,503	0	0	411,963	30,074	20,434	1,546,193	1,556,658
29	59	6,840	10,927	11,640	333,143	22,000	18,060	422,401	10,437	-1,203	1,532,845	1,543,772
30	60	6,840	11,655	11,640	344,783	0	13,020	457,587	35,186	23,546	1,542,216	1,553,871
31	61	6,657	12,447	11,457	356,240	0	7,980	494,502	36,916	25,459	1,551,821	1,564,268
32	62	6,657	13,308	11,457	367,696	0	2,940	533,178	38,676	27,219	1,561,666	1,574,974
33	63	6,657	14,229	9,457	377,153	0	0	571,566	38,388	28,931	1,569,660	1,583,889
34	64	6,657	14,963	11,457	388,610	22,000	18,060	590,618	19,052	7,596	1,556,864	1,571,826
35	65	6,657	14,801	11,457	400,066	48,000	13,020	584,073	-6,545	-18,002	1,462,713	1,477,514
36	66	6,657	14,634	11,457	411,523	48,000	7,980	576,860	-7,213	-18,669	1,369,476	1,384,110
37	67	6,657	14,420	11,457	422,980	48,000	2,940	568,981	-7,879	-19,336	1,277,016	1,291,436
38	68	6,379	14,144	9,179	432,159	48,000	0	558,043	-10,938	-20,117	1,184,928	1,199,072
39	69	6,018	13,649	10,818	442,977	70,000	18,060	524,859	-33,185	-44,003	1,074,643	1,088,292
40	70	5,684	13,346	10,484	453,461	48,000	13,020	513,739	-11,120	-21,604	990,146	1,003,493
41	71	5,367	13,619	10,167	463,628	48,000	50,773	501,087	-12,652	-22,819	957,760	971,379
42	72	5,367	13,957	10,167	473,795	48,000	90,497	489,133	-11,954	-22,121	934,639	948,596
43	73	5,367	14,343	10,167	483,962	48,000	130,222	477,950	-11,184	-21,351	911,635	925,978
44	74	5,367	14,770	10,167	494,129	48,000	169,947	467,511	-10,438	-20,605	888,818	903,588
45	75	5,367	15,181	5,367	499,496	48,000	214,712	452,716	-14,795	-20,162	861,203	876,384
46	76	5,367	16,285	5,367	504,863	48,000	259,476	439,276	-13,440	-18,807	833,792	850,077
47	77	5,367	16,805	5,367	510,229	48,000	304,241	426,613	-12,663	-18,030	807,642	824,447
48	78	5,367	17,357	5,367	515,596	48,000	349,006	414,759	-11,854	-17,221	781,816	799,174
49	79	5,367	17,927	5,367	520,963	48,000	393,771	403,724	-11,035	-16,402	756,348	774,275
50	80	5,367	18,541	5,367	526,330	48,000	438,536	393,497	-10,227	-15,594	731,246	749,787

Hypothetical & Non-Guaranteed Values

Year	Age	Total Premium	Dividend	Premium Outlay	Cum. Premium Outlay	Income	Total Loan Balance	Total Net Cash Value	Change in Total Net Cash Value	Change in Net CV Less Prem. Outlay	Total Net Death Benefit w/out Div	Total Net Death Benefit
51	81	5,367	19,204	5,367	531,697	48,000	483,300	384,056	-9,441	-14,808	706,559	725,763
52	82	5,367	19,929	5,367	537,064	48,000	528,065	375,341	-8,715	-14,082	682,340	702,269
53	83	5,367	20,677	5,367	542,431	48,000	572,830	367,342	-7,998	-13,365	658,660	679,337
54	84	5,367	21,505	5,367	547,798	48,000	617,595	360,023	-7,319	-12,686	635,534	657,039
55	85	5,367	22,399	5,367	553,165	48,000	662,359	353,317	-6,706	-12,073	613,054	635,453
56	86	5,367	23,591	5,367	558,531	48,000	707,124	347,351	-5,966	-11,333	591,291	614,882
57	87	5,367	24,563	5,367	563,898	48,000	751,889	341,719	-5,631	-10,998	570,605	595,168
58	88	5,367	25,598	5,367	569,265	48,000	796,654	336,278	-5,442	-10,808	550,714	576,312
59	89	5,367	26,677	5,367	574,632	48,000	841,419	330,863	-5,415	-10,781	531,692	558,369
60	90	5,367	27,756	5,367	579,999	48,000	886,183	325,379	-5,484	-10,851	513,596	541,353
61	91	5,367	28,816	5,367	585,366	48,000	930,948	319,749	-5,630	-10,997	496,434	525,250
62	92	5,367	29,881	5,367	590,733	48,000	975,713	314,027	-5,723	-11,090	480,193	510,074
63	93	5,367	30,865	5,367	596,100	48,000	1,020,478	308,278	-5,749	-11,115	464,891	495,756
64	94	5,367	31,767	5,367	601,466	48,000	1,065,242	302,602	-5,676	-11,043	450,446	482,213
65	95	5,367	32,504	5,367	606,833	48,000	1,110,007	297,255	-5,347	-10,714	436,774	469,278
66	96	5,367	33,627	5,367	612,200	0	1,110,007	343,503	46,247	40,881	474,466	508,093
67	97	5,367	34,976	5,367	617,567	0	1,110,007	390,943	47,440	42,073	513,126	548,103
68	98	5,367	36,310	5,367	622,934	0	1,110,007	439,625	48,683	43,316	553,006	589,316
69	99	5,367	37,706	5,367	628,301	0	1,110,007	489,645	50,020	44,653	594,087	631,793
70	100	5,367	39,152	5,367	633,668	0	1,110,007	541,260	51,615	46,248	636,442	675,595
71	101	0	40,497	0	633,668	0	1,110,007	589,612	48,352	48,352	678,857	719,354
72	102	0	41,747	0	633,668	0	1,110,007	638,683	49,071	49,071	722,521	764,268
73	103	0	43,031	0	633,668	0	1,110,007	688,500	49,817	49,817	767,340	810,371
74	104	0	44,349	0	633,668	0	1,110,007	739,164	50,664	50,664	813,358	857,707
75	105	0	45,702	0	633,668	0	1,110,007	790,848	51,684	51,684	860,620	906,322
76	106	0	47,093	0	633,668	0	1,110,007	843,961	53,112	53,112	909,167	956,260
77	107	0	48,521	0	633,668	0	1,110,007	899,361	55,401	55,401	959,033	1,007,554
78	108	0	49,987	0	633,668	0	1,110,007	956,130	56,768	56,768	1,010,232	1,060,219
79	109	0	51,493	0	633,668	0	1,110,007	1,014,303	58,173	58,173	1,062,800	1,114,293
80	110	0	53,039	0	633,668	0	1,110,007	1,073,925	59,622	59,622	1,116,777	1,169,815
81	111	0	54,626	0	633,668	0	1,110,007	1,135,032	61,107	61,107	1,172,202	1,226,828
82	112	0	56,256	0	633,668	0	1,110,007	1,197,664	62,632	62,632	1,229,118	1,285,374
83	113	0	57,930	0	633,668	0	1,110,007	1,261,870	64,206	64,206	1,287,566	1,345,496
84	114	0	59,649	0	633,668	0	1,110,007	1,327,690	65,820	65,820	1,347,589	1,407,239
85	115	0	61,415	0	633,668	0	1,110,007	1,395,172	67,482	67,482	1,409,234	1,470,649
86	116	0	63,228	0	633,668	0	1,110,007	1,464,360	69,188	69,188	1,472,546	1,535,774
87	117	0	65,090	0	633,668	0	1,110,007	1,535,304	70,944	70,944	1,537,572	1,602,662
88	118	0	67,003	0	633,668	0	1,110,007	1,608,057	72,753	72,753	1,604,361	1,671,365
89	119	0	69,318	0	633,668	0	1,110,007	1,683,013	74,956	74,956	1,672,965	1,742,282
90	120	0	71,597	0	633,668	0	1,110,007	1,760,147	77,134	77,134	1,743,791	1,815,388
91	121	0	73,707	0	633,668	0	1,110,007	1,890,508	130,361	130,361	1,816,801	1,890,508

Glossary of Terms:

Total Premium: This is the total premium due based on the on-going premium of $6,840 and the paid-up additions rider being funded for $5,000 from the emergency fund in the first four years. After the first four years the paid-up additions rider is no longer needed to be funded.

Dividend: This is the annual projected dividend paid by the insurance company based on the current dividend scale.

Premium Outlay: This is the total premium plus the loan repayments.

Cumulative Premium Outlay: This is the total of all premiums and paid up additions paid into the policy to date.

Income: This is the money that is taken out of the policy via cash value surrenders and or loans to purchase vehicles and or retirement income.

Total Loan Balance: This is the total cumulative loan balance based on borrowing against the policy for income. If the policy is not lapsed or surrendered before death this loan balance is non-taxable to the policyowner.

Total Net Cash Value: This is the total remaining cash value after all the calculations for the year are netted out.

Change in Net Cash Value: This shows the net change in total cash value for the year after all the calculations are netted out.

Total Death Benefit: This is the total remaining death benefit net of policy loans, interest and or cash value surrenders.

Tax-Free Retirement Income

In the illustration above, you will notice one other number, and that is the $48,000 a year policy loan this example takes from age 65 to age 95. That is a tax-free cash flow to the client of $48,000 a year from their policy for 30 years. The client is still saving or paying their premium in this example, but that is real tax-free retirement income.

In Summary

In this example, the client put in a cumulative $633,668. He created a system to purchase seven vehicles. He took out $1,440,000 in tax-free income and at the ripe age of 100 still has $675,595 in tax-free death benefits. That is a total cumulative benefit of $2,115,595.

So Uncommon Banking leverages your Now Money, but also provides you with that Later Money. That's the other reason we love this. The income later is like a personal pension. You can draw retirement income 100% tax-free through a return of cost basis and policy loans.

You can use your Uncommon Banking system for more than car loans. Below, we explore six other forms of residual income, most of which require cash to invest. What better way to fund that investment than from your Uncommon Banking system that has a path to replenish itself and grow with your lifestyle, needs, and entrepreneurial desires?

To sum it all up, Uncommon Banking is powerful because building wealth requires capital and liquidity. A life insurance contract designed for cash accumulation gives you multiple ways to leverage your money at the same time. As of writing this, contractually the insurance company must pay you a fixed return of 4%, and most pay a dividend on top of that. They still owe you on your cash value, even if you took a loan against it. Over time, as you build up your policy, that amount grows. The policy is also purchasing death benefits and compounding on itself as your wealth grows.

So, the multiple uses are: cash accumulation, income in the form of dividends, and a death benefit. All while being able to borrow against the cash value to purchase other assets that produce cash flow or pay off debt.

This is complicated because it is counter-intuitive to most of the things you have been taught about money. We have been doing this for families for over a decade now and understand this inside and out. At this point, you probably don't have a complete understanding of this, but if it piqued your curiosity and sounds like something you would be interested in learning more about, we have several more resources on the topic and can ultimately create custom plans for how this fits into your personal situation.

If you want to hear more on Uncommon Banking, check out our Uncommon Life Podcast Episode 6 at **https://www.uncommon wealth.com/podcasts/duocast-3**.

Cons:

It's easy to look at Uncommon Banking and wonder why everyone doesn't do this. Well, it honestly is not the best fit for every-one. Here are some things to understand as you consider using this Uncommon Banking system:

1. If you are having cash flow issues or unstable cash flow, this will feel like an expense and more of a burden than a banking system.

2. Loans are still debt, and even if the terms are more advantageous, it still feels like debt.

3. It requires a good understanding of your budget and plan so debt does not become a burden.

4. This is not a get-rich-quick scheme. It is a very long-term plan requiring a level of patience.

5. You may not qualify based on your health or past due to underwriting requirements.

6. It has been our experience that if you cannot do at least $10,000 a year in premium with ample cushion, financially you are not ready for this strategy.

CHAPTER 9

Investing in the Seven Sources of Residual Income: Real Estate, Investments, and Business

SOURCE 2: Real Estate

Dovetailing off Uncommon Banking, real estate is one of the more popular sources of residual income for wealth creation, because it also offers multiple ways for you to build wealth. Let's look at them.

First, you receive rental income. So you do your research and find an ideal rental property. When you make the down payment and are at the settlement table, you own the full asset value of that property. You charge rent based on the full price, not on what you have put down on the property. For example, if you buy a duplex for $200,000, but only put $40,000 as a down payment, you still charge rent based on the $200,000 value of the duplex to your tenants. So, the first use of rental property is profit from rent or rental income that exceeds your expenses.

The second is the equity accrual or equity built up in the home by using that rental income to pay the mortgage. The third way to build wealth with real estate is capital appreciation. Over time, a well-maintained property can appreciate, building you even more wealth. We explore real estate on a regular basis. Our podcast, conversations, work with clients, and many articles we write often focus on real estate. There are so many ways to create cash flow, build wealth, and hedge against inflation with plays in real estate.

Exploring Real Estate Sectors

Let's look at the different categories of real estate at a high level and then break down options from there. We don't want to overwhelm you with ideas, but it is important to understand the landscape and avenues of real estate at a high level. Often when we have these conversations, people don't realize all the avenues available to explore real estate investments.

Real estate can be divided into four main categories: Residential, Commercial, Industrial, and Land. The first two are the most typical, so we'll focus on those, but also touch on industrial real estate and land.

Residential real estate has multiple sub-categories. There are single family homes from humble abodes to executive rentals, targeting the more affluent. For example, Des Moines, Iowa, has a lot of insurance companies, and many times, executives will move to Des Moines and want to rent for a year or two because they want to either explore the region before they buy, or they might be moving on to another position in the near future.

Then you have duplexes, triplexes, and quadplexes. These are multiple units attached with shared walls, but have unique addresses and living spaces for each unit. The reason we group these together is because you can purchase a quadplex on a conventional 30-year mortgage with only one loan. Once you go above four units, or a quadplex, then you are moving into a commercial loan.

There are hybrid real estate categories that still fit into the overall residential category. Airbnb and VRBO have become extremely popular worldwide, and their popularity is another subject we cover often in podcasts, articles, and conversations with clients. Typically done through single-family homes, condos, and town-homes, they fall under primary mortgages, and can generate income like a hotel would.

Next you have **commercial real estate**. If you purchase beyond a quadplex apartment building, you are moving into commercial real estate. Because you are providing services to so many people, you are basically running a business, hence the commercial classification. Lending occurs through a commercial loan for commercial real estate.

Hotels, which are providing short-term stays and also act as a for-profit business to provide the service, require commercial financing. Notice the distinct difference here. There are two cash flows. One for the rent for owning the building and another for the the revenue generated by the hotel operator.

Most commercial real estate loans are built on 20-year mortgages, not 30, and require a refinance or balloon payment every five years to reduce the risk to the bank.

Another favorite of ours in the commercial real estate space is mobile home parks. On our podcast, Caleb Walsh talks about his experience with mobile home parks and how he has grown his portfolio. Phillip's family also owns a mobile home park in Nebraska, so we are somewhat familiar with these. Although you need a commercial loan to purchase a mobile home park, it serves the residential market. You own the land, and the tenants in the park pay rent to stay on your land. You can also sell trailers and upgrade units to make additional money.

Caleb's incredible story does not stop there. With less than $10,000 in the bank, credit card debt up to his eyeballs, credit scores in the toilet, and his wife pregnant with their first child, he had the dream of owning apartment buildings. You see the challenge. There was no war chest to get this "battle for building a dream" started.

Now he is a leading authority in affordable housing with portfolios spanning over 1,500 units in six states.

Not everyone has as dramatic a story as his, but we all have dreams, and money is often a key ingredient to making those dreams come true.

If you want to hear more about Caleb's story, check out our Uncommon Life Project Podcast, Episode 11 at **https://www.uncom monwealth.com/podcasts/caleb-walsh**. Chris Ramsey (Phillip's mom) also owns a mobile home park with her sisters. Hear her story at **https://www.uncommonwealth.com/podcasts/chris-ramsey.**

Other examples of commercial real estate include strip malls, corporate centers, and most other types of business operations that use real estate to operate.

The exception is **industrial real estate**. These are larger operations such as manufacturing or distribution like an Amazon fulfillment warehouse. Other examples would be chemical, pharmaceutical, agricultural, and petrochemical operations.

The last category is **land**. As the saying goes, "God isn't making any more of it." Buying land is great if you are building a home, but buying land for commercial reasons and erecting buildings, neighborhoods, and developing communities is big business and carries lots of risk. Land development requires long-term strategy and a lot of cash. Because it can take a long time to generate cash flow, land development carries more risk than other types of real estate investments. They call it land speculation for a reason.

From Dipping a Toe to Diving In

When it comes to building residual income, real estate is an avenue that has a low barrier to entry. We often suggest dipping a toe in, like Phillip did in 2019. He and his wife decided to put their primary residence on Airbnb. You can literally earn some residual income while you vacation when you put up your own home on Airbnb. This isn't for everyone, but it is a way of testing the waters in real estate. If you are interested in that story, listen to Episode 45 of the Uncommon Life Project at **https://www.uncommonwealth.com/podcasts/duocast-16**.

The next step would be to purchase investment property, for short or long-term rental. Here again, you can start small, with one property. But there are so many ways you can leverage this one property. If you are in a college town, you can rent out individual rooms for more than you could charge for one family to rent it as a single residence. You could go the Airbnb route and do short-term rentals, for potentially more than you could get per month from a single renter. You could purchase a duplex or quadplex.

If you put systems in place for collecting rent and managing the property, you can keep going and purchase multiple homes or even apartment buildings. You can leverage the properties you own to purchase others and grow a portfolio of as many buildings as makes sense for you and your situation.

The great thing is, this is Now Money, not money hidden away in a financial instrument you can't touch without penalty before age 60. You can build toward Money and Time Freedom (retirement) while also generating residual income for those dreams you have right now.

Other Pros:

Here are some other benefits to real estate as a source of residual income that are worth noting:

1. You have a tangible asset you can physically drive by or see.

2. The U.S. Tax Code is tailored to owning real estate, making capital investments, and hiring.

3. You can leverage other people's money by taking a loan from the bank through a mortgage.

4. Real Estate is one of the best ways to fight inflation inherent in our monetary system because you can borrow at fixed rates on residential mortgages and you can increase rent over time, which also protects your purchasing power over time.

Cons:

1. Real estate takes time and management to scale and find opportunities. Do you really have the time to invest?

2. Leverage can go both ways; borrowing money creates risk if you can't get the property rented.

3. Real estate and rentals do have codes and regulations. Complying with ordinances and regulations can reduce profit, take time you may not have, and limit potential uses of the property. For example, many cities and townships are enacting their own local short-term rental laws to restrict the impact of Airbnb and VRBO.

4. Maintenance is real. Properties that are being rented require upkeep and investment to maintain the asset value of the property. Maintenance funds should be budgeted in ahead of time.

5. Interest rates have been historically low for the last 20 years and look like they could be into the future, but rising interest rates increase mortgage expenses and put pressure on property values.

6. Location, location, location is vitally important to your real estate, and the more you pay, the more critical it can be.

SOURCE 3: Investments

For us, when we speak about investments, we are talking about putting your money to work through the stock and bond markets, foreign currency, Bitcoin and cryptocurrency, and futures markets. Today there are so many different types of accounts, brokerage firms, and investment vehicles that it can be hard to navigate your way through.

In this section, we want to make the distinction like we did earlier between saving and investing. We want to make the distinction between investing, speculating, and trading. Each of these is a very different thing. As we noted in Chapter 6, there are many different types of accounts or registrations you can use to invest. This section explores the different things you can invest in and the high-level philosophies that give you a broader view of the investment world.

Investing in its simplest form is putting your money into a company's shares, index, or bond, whether it be pre-tax or after-tax, in order to generate a return or growth on your money. Your time horizon is beyond three years of needing that money, and you are willing to take some risk for the potential of a return. You are going to stick with the strategy you are choosing even if the value goes down.

Modern-Portfolio Theory

Modern Portfolio Theory (MPT) argues that it's possible to design an ideal portfolio that will provide the investor maximum returns by taking on the optimal amount of risk. This is the foundation of traditional financial advising in America and can also be interchanged with the term "asset allocation."

In particular, MPT advocates diversification of securities and asset classes, or the benefits of not putting all your eggs in one basket. This would be where your portfolio holds large cap mutual funds, mid cap, small cap, international, corporate bonds, and government bonds as well as some commodities and real estate. MPT says stocks face both systematic risk—market risks such as interest rates and recessions—as well as unsystematic risk—issues that are specific to each stock such as management changes or poor sales. MPT believes that proper diversification of a portfolio can't prevent systematic risk, but it can dampen, if not eliminate, unsystematic risk.

Buy and Hold

Buy and Hold is more of a generic term for buying either individual stocks, bonds, mutual funds, or exchange traded funds and accumulating a position over time, reinvesting dividends, and not rotating or selling your holdings. This is very similar to passive investing.

Indexing or Passive Investing

Indexing, or passive investing, is a strategy designed to match a market, not beat it. Done properly, it can be cheap and tax efficient.

After costs and taxes, an indexed investor in a market can beat the average active investor.

Tactical

Tactical asset management responds to market conditions. It looks at the present and the near future. A tactical investor attempts to shift or rotate the composition of a portfolio to reduce risk exposure or to take advantage of accelerating data within the economy or a sub sector of the markets. This is a data-driven approach looking for accelerating and decelerating information on lots of different asset classes. Where modern portfolio theory and traditional asset allocation change the weighting of a portfolio but still maintain exposure to most asset classes, tactical money managers look to exit asset classes entirely depending on the market conditions and data they are interpreting.

Active Management

Active management is where a money manager or investment manager is actively buying and selling securities to try and beat the index of a basket of stocks. The core belief is that with access to information, research, and due diligence, the manager can beat the underlying index he is benchmarked to and can create return beyond buying and holding. An example of this would be a large cap mutual fund manager. His underlying benchmark might be the S&P 500, but instead of mirroring that index, he would overweight the securities he liked, trying to beat the performance of the S&P 500.

Fees

There are traditionally four layers of fees:

Asset Management Fees: the fees that are charged by the company, firm, or investment institution making, buying, and selling decisions within the portfolio you are invested in.

Advisory Fees: these are the fees paid to the advisor to set up, manage, and review the portfolio with you, the client.

Trading Fees: these are the fees the brokerage firm charged for trades to be placed.

Administrative Fees: these are fees for complying with government rules and regulations and the administration of your account including statements.

Investment Objectives

Growth investing or investments largely don't pay dividends and are focused on growing the value of your investment versus collecting income in the form of dividends. Growth stocks and investments typically have more volatility or ups and downs and are characterized by higher potential returns helping you accumulate wealth faster.

Income investing is largely focusing on investments that pay income or a return of a company's cash-flow to mitigate the risk of investing and giving someone else your capital. This looks like either buying bonds in a company versus their stock or receiving dividends or preferred dividends if you own preferred stock. The goal of income investing is to create or generate passive income while staying invested. So the focus is more current income and less capital appreciation, whereas growth focuses more on capital appreciation and less on current income.

The 4% Rule: The main premise of investing has largely been to grow your money while you are young to build up balances across the various types of accounts we highlighted in Chapter 6 (Roth IRA, Traditional IRA, 401(k), After-Tax Brokerage, etc.), and then once that balance was big enough, you could start withdrawing income from that portfolio into perpetuity. The 4% rule basically says that you can withdraw 4% of the entire balance of your account annually without running out of money based on a normal 60% stock or equity holding and 30% bond holdings and 10% in treasury holdings.

So if you need $7,500 a month off your investments, that is $90,000 a year and at a 4% withdrawal rate, you would need a balance of $2,250,000. You would take $90,000 divided by .04 (4%), and that is how you come up with $2,250,000. Those are really the basics of financial planning advice.

Speculating is putting your money into something you don't understand one time for the potential of making above-average returns. Typically, this results in a loss and can be painful and financially and emotionally harmful. This is counter to our philosophy which is predicated more on investing in things you know and are passionate about.

Trading is the creation, testing, and following of a system that should generate a profitable trade more than 50% of the time. Trading is a profession or day job where you are systematically trading your account to generate above-average return.

In order to trade successfully, you need a supported environment to learn and be mentored in. You must do your own research and practice, practice, practice. Trading is emotional, and we recommend trading with fake money for months before putting your own money into play.

Another way to gain confidence in your trading strategy is called **back testing**. Back testing is the process of going back in history to see how your trading strategy would have performed in the past. The more back testing you do, the more you can understand how your strategy performs in different kinds of markets. This is not an indication of the future, but it will help you to gain the confidence you need.

Once you are confident and feel like you are ready, trading can be fun and easy, more now than it has ever been, because you can make money from within the comfort of your home. Once you understand your process and have a history of how it would perform, you can literally profit from anywhere in the world. It is not passive in the sense that you are not doing anything. Quite the contrary. It takes a lot of practice, skill, and attention, but once you learn what you're doing, it can be a great way to generate income without working for someone else. Between equity markets, indices, options futures, foreign exchanges, and cryptocurrency markets, you can literally trade from anywhere in the world, 24/7.

The four keys to trading are:

- Find a strategy that you are comfortable with that matches your time availability to trade.

- Have a mentor to teach you and practice with.

- Back test.

- Practice, practice, practice by documenting and trading by the rules you have set with "paper money."

Cons:

Investing and Trading are great until you lose money. The cons of trading and investing are:

1. You can lose all your money.

2. Where your money goes, so does your time and attention. This goes for everything, but we bring it up here because the market doesn't sleep. Unlike the market value of your rental property, you don't receive monthly statements in the mail like you do with your investment accounts. Seeing the market value of your investments change daily can be unnerving or distracting for certain people.

3. Taxes for short-term capital gains can eat into returns.

4. You need to be able to handle the emotions of investing and trading as history has shown the markets can and will go down at different times.

5. You don't really know what is going on inside of publicly traded companies—think Enron, WorldCom, etc.

SOURCE 4: Business

Wait, this is a chapter about residual income. How does business fit into that? Starting a business is anything but simple. There's not a magic wand to wave to get a business off the ground, with you just sitting back and letting the profits flow.

When it comes to starting your own business, building residual income is playing the long game. It doesn't happen overnight. But in our experience, there is no one source of income that can provide income in as many ways as a business can. One business can provide income in many of these other categories, like real estate, licensing, and subscription models.

This sounds complicated and scary, but it doesn't need to be. Building a business is a great way to create several streams of income. It certainly won't feel residual when you start out, but the idea is to develop a business you can step away from or sell at some point.

Starting a business is an investment. The rewards that have come with starting our business have been both awesome and humbling. The lives we have touched and those who have touched us have been priceless.

Okay, let's get down to it. How does a business help build residual income? We see five main ways.

1. Generating or replacing your salary from leaving employment with someone else.

2. You can provide employment to others, so you can leverage other peoples' time, talents, and gifts to produce more than what you could do on your own.

3. Capital: If you can invest your capital and provide a finished good that sells at a good profit margin, you can generate an above-average return on your capital.

4. In business, you can borrow money from investors or a bank at a lower rate. If you are able to take that money and generate a gross profit of, say, 50% and a net profit of, say, 15% over time, you can expand faster and make even more wealth.

5. If you input systems and procedures so your business can run without you, then you have something of value to sell to another potential business owner. When the business is not dependent on you, the value increases. That's called capital appreciation.

Christina Moffatt comes to mind as someone who took a passion and turned it into a business. During the economic meltdown of 2008-2009, she started bringing treats into work to help ease the anxiety everyone was feeling. She then leveraged that into a successful business and even made a television appearance on *Cupcake Wars*. Christina is now in a leadership role for an organization focused on helping small businesses all over Iowa and still owns her company. If you want to hear more about her story and the challenges along the way, listen to Episode 39 of the Uncommon Life Project. **https://www.uncommonwealth.com/podcasts/christina-moffatt**

Let's define what a business is. A business is a corporate structure that uses economic resources (time, people, technology, real estate, and capital) to provide goods or services to customers in exchange for money.

There are three main business types that we want to home in on within this chapter.

Service Business—A service type of business provides intangible products or solutions to customers (products with no physical form). Service-related businesses offer professional skills, expertise, advice, and other similar services as their product.

Some examples of service businesses would be: massage and spas, automotive shops, financial advisors, accounting firms, counseling or coaching firms, plumbers, and electricians.

Merchandising or Retail Business—These types of businesses buy products at wholesale prices and sell the same products at a marked-up retail price to the public. They make profit by selling a large volume of products at prices higher than the costs to purchase those goods and the fixed costs of operating the business. Instead of selling on volume, these businesses can also sell fewer higher-end goods that retail at a much higher price, generating a larger profit per transaction or customer.

A merchandising business sells a product without changing its form. Examples are: grocery stores, convenience stores, distributors, and other resellers—think Walmart, Target, and Amazon.

Manufacturing Business—A manufacturing business buys inputs or raw materials with the intention of using them in making an entirely new product. There is a proprietary process that has been created to craft or create an entirely new product for the marketplace.

A manufacturing business combines these raw materials, labor from its employees, and overhead costs of accounting, facilities, power, and technology in its production process. The manufactured goods will then be sold directly to customers or to merchandising businesses that will then sell the final product to the end customer.

Examples would be car manufacturers, appliance manufacturers, food manufacturers, and clothing companies.

Hybrids—Hybrid businesses are companies that may be classified as more than one type of business. A restaurant, for example, combines ingredients in making a meal (manufacturing), sells beer and wine (merchandising), and fills customer orders for appetizers, meals, and desserts (service).

This is a big reason why we broke out in our Seven Sources of Residual Income the Subscription Model and Affiliate Businesses because they are almost their own sub-class or category of business. Further, utilizing your intellectual property is another form of business without necessarily having to start a business. The same goes for network marketing. They allow you to partner with businesses, but not take on the full risk or responsibility of owning a business. We will cover those more as we progress through the book. Business is a large category and just the word can carry a lot of weight and connotation to people.

Business Organizational Structures

These are the basic forms of how a business can legally structure itself in the United States.

Sole Proprietor—A sole proprietorship is a business owned by only one person. It is easy to set up and is the least costly among all forms of ownership. The owner faces unlimited liability, meaning the creditors of the business may go after the personal assets of the owner if the business cannot pay them.

The sole proprietorship form is usually adopted by small business entities.

Partnership (LP, LLP)—A partnership is a business owned by two or more persons who contribute resources into the entity. The partners divide the profits of the business among themselves.

In general partnerships, all partners have unlimited

liability. In limited partnerships, creditors cannot go after the personal assets of the limited partners.

Limited Liability Company (LLC)—Limited liability companies (LLCs) in the U.S., are hybrid forms of business that have characteristics of both a corporation and a partnership. An LLC is not incorporated. Hence, it is not considered a corporation. But the owners enjoy limited liability like in a corporation. An LLC may elect to be taxed as a sole proprietorship, a partnership, or a corporation.

Corporation (S-Corp, C-Corp)—A corporation is a business organization that has a separate legal personality from its owners. Ownership in a stock corporation is represented by shares of stock.

The owners (stockholders) enjoy limited liability but have limited involvement in the company's operations. The board of directors, an elected group from the stockholders, controls the activities of the corporation.

In addition to those basic forms of business ownership, these are some other types of organizations that are common today:

Cooperative or Co-Op—A cooperative is a business organization owned by a group of individuals and is operated for their mutual benefit. The persons making up the group are called members. Cooperatives may be incorporated or unincorporated.

Some examples of cooperatives are: water and electricity (utility) cooperatives, cooperative banking, credit unions, and housing cooperatives.

In any business, you have the challenge of letting your ideal customers know that you are in business and open. The landscape of business is changing so fast, and technology is progressing so quickly, that the job of a business to tell its story and educate and connect with its clients and fans is requiring the business owner to adapt. We wanted to include this in this chapter because it has helped us look at our business differently, and lots of our clients are resonating with it.

Client Education Strategy—Setting Up the Value Ladder

We've come to see this as an incredibly important aspect of launching and sustaining a business. Client education is a strategic way to assert yourself as a subject-matter expert. When you find your niche, you've got to create a clear pathway for people to get to know you, understand your expertise, and want to do business with you.

It starts with a "value ladder." This is one of the things we wish we would have understood earlier in the process of starting our business, which is why we talk about it so passionately. It helps people step into your unique process or products and services.

When we first started our business, we were eager to help. We were excited about what we had to offer and wanted everyone to get as much benefit as possible. So in those early days, we gave a lot of intellectual property away for free, without setting up a process for people to climb up the ladder with us from helpful, less expensive stuff to our highest-value resources at a correspondingly higher price.

Several years in, we wanted to write a book and had a lot to say, but it was not fully organized and refined yet. We started writing one-page articles on smaller topics, and that really helped us galvanize our message over time. Now, we have written our book, and the organization of ideas and the Uncommon Wealth Path we are rolling out is a by-product of writing more than 200 articles and establishing our unique process after meeting with hundreds of families and studying those who have the most success financially.

That's what the value ladder is all about. This book is a prime example of a first step on the ladder which is not pictured. The image below is of a generic value ladder, not our specific one. For us, though, our free content or "freemium," as it is called, consisted of the articles, podcasts, our YouTube channel, and our newsletter. Hopefully, many will find it helpful, some will be curious about what other products or services we provide, and a few will move up the ladder.

If you do not set up a value ladder, you are likely to give away too much for free or for too little monetary value. You want to create an experience of people gaining more in exchange for a higher price point. The illustration below shows how this might progress.

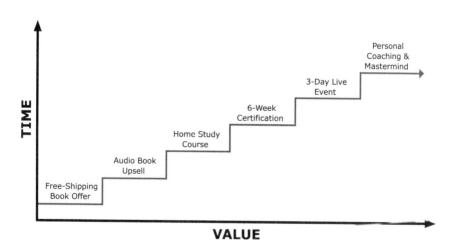

Franchises

Franchises are a great sub-sector of business because they are a proven formula for generating revenue and delivering a consistent product or service. Franchises also allow passionate owners to focus on the part of the business they like and rely on existing systems and hiring practices to help solidify other aspects of the business they may struggle with. Some of those functions that come to mind are accounting, human resources, or inventory.

Franchises also provide scale, as the business is part of something larger which can help with brand awareness, technology applications, and national advertising. Lots of people we meet love business, but the thought of creating everything from scratch can be overwhelming. Franchises provide proven tracks to run on.

Business can be all these things and provide a huge reward:

- Although challenging, it can be part of your legacy that you leave to others.

- It can help you impact many people: from the people you are serving as your clients to the people you employ.

- It is something you can always improve, make more efficient, and learn from.

If you are a business owner, you have some tremendous wealth-building tools at your disposal that you might not even be aware of. Think of your ability to build wealth as a 5-pointed star.

5-Star Wealth—How a Business Can Fuel Multiple Ways to Build Wealth

Imagine you are a chiropractor running your own practice. Your business itself is the first point on the star. You help people have the healthiest spine and frame they can possibly have, and they pay you for your knowledge and expertise. You have a thriving business.

When considering the potential for wealth-building, this is just the starting point. This is an important mindset shift to make as we consider the many ways you can build on what you are earning in the business itself.

The second point on the star is liquidity. Any business owner knows that to be successful, you must have ready access to cash. A large portion of the 95% of businesses that fail can attribute that failure to a lack of liquidity or access to capital. So to unlock your savings and true compound interest, we look toward our Uncommon Banking strategy. For this, you would establish a cash-value life insurance policy, which is 100% contractually guaranteed, tax-deferred, and liquid for your flexibility and convenience while supporting a death benefit and rate of return on your money. There are other ways to maintain liquidity, but the benefits of Uncommon Banking make this our first suggestion in this category.

A business and liquidity are great, but we are just getting started. The third point on that star of wealth creation is home ownership. You and your family need to sleep somewhere, so home ownership is a logical step. Paying that mortgage builds equity within your home and is one more way to build wealth.

There are so many ways real estate can help you build wealth, which brings us to the fourth point on the star. Let's say you own the building where your chiropractic office is located. There are two potential ways to benefit from rental income when you own the building where you run your business. If the building is large enough, you can rent space to other tenants. It's a great source of wealth building. But even without tenants, you can take advantage of owning that building. We suggest paying rent to yourself through your own LLC, a separate entity that owns the building. There are tax advantages to setting up the LLC and paying rent to yourself this way. Let's say your chiropractic business is set up as an S-Corp, which pays rent to the LLC that owns the building. This is not considered wages, so it does not involve payroll tax. It is a way to get income out of your business and into your other pocket in a more tax-advantaged state. The building can be depreciated, which can also help you on your tax liability.

These four wealth-building points are exciting on their own, but you should also have a fifth point on the star.

That would be a retirement plan. We don't suggest putting all your eggs in this basket, but having money in a retirement plan does provide for a tax deduction, and it is one more resource for you as you age. Access is deferred until retirement age, but that money will be there for you as another source of income when the time comes. It also acts as a recruiting tool for future employees as they have the ability to contribute and be matched for their retirement.

This 5-pointed star analogy demonstrates why business owners often build wealth faster than those who don't own a business. You can literally be building wealth in five different ways at the same time, whereas most employees are typically only building wealth through a retirement plan and their home equity.

We hope this gets your wheels turning as you consider your options. You have more wealth-building potential than you realize. Take full advantage of these five points to help you along the Uncommon Path.

Cons:

1. 95% of all businesses fail.

2. It is like giving birth and raising a child, and if not done properly, it can really go wrong.

3. It can consume your time and energy if you don't know how

to set boundaries and scale the operations and systems to protect your time.

4. It can cost you lots of money if not done properly and expose you to more liability as you sell products and services to more and more people.

5. It can rob you of the joy you once felt when you started if you don't take care of it and create systems and processes to keep you in your sweet spot.

CHAPTER 10

Investing in the Seven Sources of Residual Income: Subscription Model and Affiliate Income, Intellectual Property, and Network Marketing

SOURCE 5: Subscription Model and Affiliate Income

The subscription model is all around us. We participate in multiple ways every day. You head to the gym over lunch. It's an upper-body day. Later, when you get home, a box from Stitch Fix is waiting on the front porch. After dinner, you catch up with the latest episodes of that show about dragons/midwives/spies or whatever you're watching on Netflix these days, as the kids listen to Spotify and your spouse has a glass of wine from her wine-of-the-month club.

What if you could use a subscription model in your business to smooth out your revenue with more predictable cash flow? What if, in doing so, you developed more loyal fans who appreciated the predictability of regular payments for access to the services they love? Your business may be in a great position to offer a subscription model. Would that predictability and growth potential make a difference in your work?

That is the power of subscriptions. Let's take a closer look at just a few variations on the subscription model.

- **The Network Model**—The network model is as common as Facebook, WhatsApp, and multi-user video games. The value of the network model goes up the more participants there are in that network.

- **The Surprise Box Model**—We have come a long way from the Jelly-of-the-Month club. Now you can get a surprise box of clothing, clothing accessories, any beverage you can imagine, and pet care delivered right to your doorstep. You get the picture. This is a clearly defined and passionate group of customers interested in a category of goods.

- **The Private Club Model**—Exclusivity is the draw here. If you have something in limited supply that people are willing to pay a premium for, the private club model is something to consider. It might be a literal club, like a country club, yacht club or the like. It also might be an association of similar business owners.

- **The Front-of-the-Line Model**—When premium pricing gives you quicker access to problem-solving or greater resources, this is the front-of-the-line model at work. For instance, Salesforce offers memberships to all for a certain monthly fee, but a premium membership gets you faster access to support for mission-critical issues.

- **The Membership Website Model**—This one has lots of potential for niche markets who are looking for ongoing education about an area of interest. This can be in-depth industry news or education. Bloomberg offers premium access to business news behind a paywall. MarketingProfs offers access to training and education and reduced pricing for online and in-person conferences for people in that line of work.

• **The Simplifier Model**—These days, it seems that anything can be provided with the modifier, "as a service." That's because providing specific areas of expertise as a service means simplifying the lives of other people. This is a big deal in the business-to-business (B2B) market, where you can subscribe to get IT, AV, and any technical expertise you can imagine as a service for an agreed-upon price per month. This model is making inroads in the business-to-consumer (B2C) market as well. A great example is Hassle Free Homes, where for a monthly fee, all your to-do list projects can be handled, from changing HVAC filters to replacing shower/tub caulk. Sounds like heaven to us!

Affiliate Income

Affiliate marketing is a marketing arrangement by which an online retailer pays commission to individuals or companies who promote their product or service. It is a way for a company to sell its products by signing up individuals or companies ("affiliates") who market the company's products for a commission. For people who are naturally good at sales, it can be an excellent source of residual income.

There are companies out there that will pay you to recommend their product to your sphere of influence. This source of residual income is not for everyone, but there are many people who are getting paid well for their relationships and the personal brand that they have created. If you want to hear more about the influencer economy and the potential for affiliate income, listen to Episode 33 of our podcast with the one and only Stacy Jones of Hollywood Branded who helps companies all over the world do this very thing. **https://www. uncommonwealth.com/podcasts/stacy-jones**.

Cons:

1. Subscription models require a lot of effort over a long period of time. So think about this as a game you want to play for years.

2. Affiliate marketing or influencer marketing requires you to stay current on technology and social media-driven content, information, and engagement, which can cost time and money.

3. You have to stay ahead of the curve and be constantly innovating and creating new value, which can become daunting if you aren't careful or ready to handle it.

SOURCE 6: Intellectual Property

If you have ideas, products, or other kinds of intellectual property that you have developed or would like to develop, these can be a true source of residual income where you create something one time, and the income keeps coming in over time. That's what can happen when you protect your intellectual property through patents, trademarks, or copyrights.

Patents—The need for a patent is usually obvious. You develop something unique, and you want to be able to reap the rewards of that development without having others steal the idea and run with it in the marketplace. A patent protects you by excluding others from making, using, selling, or importing an invention. It gives you legal recourse when others violate the patent provisions.

Patents can generate income through a business developed to include a product with the patented idea. If manufacturing is not something you are prepared to do, the patent can also generate residual income by enabling you to enlist someone else to produce and sell your invention while providing you with a set percentage of the income from the patent on that invention.

Trademarks—Trademarks are important because without them, your business name, logo, slogan, and brand awareness (that helps people recognize your business out there in the market-place) are up for grabs.

Let's start with the basics. What is a trademark? According to the US Patent and Trademark Office:

> *"A trademark is a word, name, symbol, or device that is used in trade with goods to indicate the source of the goods and to distinguish them from the goods of others. A service mark is the same as a trademark except that it identifies and distinguishes the source of a service rather than a product. The terms 'trademark' and 'mark' are commonly used to refer to both trademarks and service marks."*

So trademarks protect brand names, slogans, and logos. The legal process of trademarking exists to send out a formal notice that a business is declaring exclusive rights to a name.

Copyrights—Why should you bother concerning yourself with copyright law? Bottom line: you do not want people stealing your stuff. For the same reason you lock up your office at night and use other security measures for your physical property, you want to protect the intellectual property held in your business. Copyright laws are one way of protecting that intellectual property.

With that in mind, here are a few things entrepreneurs should understand about copyright laws and what you can do to protect and benefit from your intellectual property.

- A copyright protects creative work that has been "fixed in a tangible medium of expression." In other words, it's not just the creative idea itself, but the idea put down in writing, sound, or image.

- A copyright is not forever. United States Copyright law stipulates that intellectual property created after 1978 is copyrighted for the life of the creator, plus 70 years.

- Copyright law covers books, movies, sound recordings, blog posts, emails, drawings, photographs, and even computer code. Pretty much anything that can be described as a tangible medium of expression.

- Copyright registration is not necessary, but it can save you some headaches. Copyright is technically granted from the moment you create something. But by registering the copyright, you have clear legal recourse and can more easily collect statutory damages and attorney's fees in the event of litigation around that copyright. Rule of thumb: any time you have a work that you think will be valuable in the future, or that has clearly shown value, it's probably time to go ahead and register that work.

• You do not need a lawyer to register a copyright. You can do it right now through the U.S. Copyright Office. For more than one registration, or if you have more than one creator attached to the intellectual property or similar complication, consulting a lawyer familiar with copyright law might be in your best interest.

Copyright law grants copyright owners six exclusive rights:

1. To reproduce (make copies of) the copyrighted work.

2. To prepare new versions and adaptations of your original copyrighted work (this is also known as the derivative work right).

3. To publicly distribute the copyrighted work.

4. To publicly perform the copyrighted work.

5. To publicly display the copyrighted work.

6. To digitally perform copyrighted sound recordings.

Here is the upshot: registering a copyright makes ownership crystal clear. Only the copyright holder has a right to use a copyrighted work. All others must seek permission from the owner to use a copyrighted work. Copyright law also stipulates monetary penalties for using someone's copyrighted work without permission. Fines are based on a court determination of financial damage to the copyright holder.

If your work is copyrighted in the U.S., international treaties provide protection for copyrighted work in most countries around the world.

The law provides some amount of insight into copyright

ownership in complex situations. Business owners should be aware of one complication in copyright law regarding "works for hire." If an employee creates website content, a brochure, or code used in the business' proprietary software, for example, the copyright is generally held by the business and not the individual employee.

Is it a perfect system? No. Led Zeppelin has been in court for several years over their song "Stairway to Heaven" with no resolution as of this writing. An otherwise forgettable 1960s-era band called Spirit had produced a song entitled "Taurus" prior to the release of "Stairway to Heaven," and a section of "Taurus" sounds remarkably similar to the intro to "Stairway to Heaven." Spirit sued in 2014, and the case was thought to be settled, but it returned in 2018 for retrial.

Things in copyright law can get pretty funky, and having a registered copyright is not a guarantee of a perfect outcome, but it will protect your intellectual property from outright theft. As we will explore in the next paragraph, it can also bring financial reward through the beautiful art of licensing. In this way, authors, musicians, artists, coders, and others can license the use of their copyrighted works as a means of earning income from their creations.

Monetizing Your Intellectual Property

In order to monetize your intellectual assets through royalties and other vehicles, protecting that property through patent, trademark, copyright, and licensing should be your default position. There is a lot to lose if you don't.

We have seen entrepreneurs create a brand, buy a website, and start generating revenue, only to receive a cease and desist order from a larger entity that has a similar brand, name, product, or service. That company had the legal protection of copyrights, trademarks, and legally protected intellectual property to back their order up. Without the actual legal protection for your property in hand, your recourse is extremely limited.

> **Licensing**—Licensing puts the responsibility of production and/or distribution on someone else. This is usually someone who has a greater capacity to get production and distribution up and running. While licensing does not guarantee showers of money will start flowing down on you, there are three distinct advantages to licensing:
>
> 1. Get your product or service to market faster.
>
> 2. Benefit from better margins than if you had tried to do it yourself.
>
> 3. Working with a larger company provides protection for your idea because they have a vested interest in your success.

If you want to listen to more on Intellectual Property, we shot an amazing podcast with Matthew Leaper where he reviews these topics in depth in Episode 36: **https://www.uncommonwealth .com/podcasts/matthew-leaper**

Cons:

1. Protecting intellectual property can cost a lot of money up front, with no guarantee of recouping those losses.

2. Enforcing your patent, trademark, or copyright is just as important as getting one. You need to actively use your intellectual property to enforce it.

SOURCE 7: Network Marketing

Network marketing is a way for a company to sell directly to consumers, with a compensation structure based on selling products as well as recruiting new distributors.

You join a distributorship, sell a product, and recruit new distributors who become your "downline."

The power of network marketing comes from your personal network and your ability to duplicate leadership. In talking with friends and family through your daily interactions and your social media presence, the products you are selling—whether they are science-based toys for toddlers or vitamin supplements for older adults—might strike a chord with people in your networks. The freedom of creating your own schedule around another job or just your day-to-day life is also an attraction of network marketing.

Your downline is created when people join your distribution network under you, creating revenue for themselves and providing you with a percentage of those sales. You become part of their "upline."

With each new distributor you recruit to your network, you start to build your downline. Each of your recruits, in turn, are taught the benefits of recruiting new distributors to their network, and in doing so, your downline structure continues to grow.

The start-up costs can be relatively low compared to starting and launching your own business. For entrepreneurs who are light on cash, network marketing can be a great way to start building something and be around like-minded people.

If you want to hear more from people who are considered professional network marketers, check out these podcasts:

Episode 9 – **https://www.uncommonwealth.com/podcasts/doug-shiplett**

Episode 24 – **https://www.uncommonwealth.com/podcasts/
rashard-adaeze-duncan/**

Cons:

1. Some people have a negative interpretation of people who do network marketing, multi-level marketing, etc.

2. Companies can be untruthful and change the compensation structure, stop paying their people, and/or deliver lower-quality products than what is promised.

3. If you are not equipped interpersonally or relationally, it can make relationships awkward when you go out to recruit family and friends.

4. It's a lot of work and takes the right type of mindset.

5. The government is starting to look more and more at this space and requiring more disclosures, more regulation, and even shutting down opportunities, thus wiping out all that you have worked for.

No Juggling Required

The point of all these sources of income is not to overwhelm you. It is to show you what is possible. Everything we do and discuss to help people with their financial picture starts with understanding them.

What makes you tick? What are you passionate about? What we help people do is to find that sweet spot where their passion fulfills a need in the marketplace.

Building residual income-producing assets is not simple. It doesn't happen overnight. But by building on your own strengths and assets as a human being, you can build cash flow that starts now and follows you through retirement age using your Now Money.

There is another great way to learn more about these sources of residual income. For an audio dive into this topic, take a listen to our podcast episode on the subject:

https://www.uncommonwealth.com/podcasts/duocast-2

A Glimpse Down the Uncommon Path:

Adrian Brambila – The Dancing Entrepreneur

We wanted to highlight someone in this chapter who went down the Uncommon Path and never looked back. Someone who earned multiple sources of income and has a story that starts from the ground up.

Adrian Brambila was the first person in his family to go to college. After his first semester of not doing so hot and feeling guilty for all that his parents had worked for and sacrificed to get him there, he wanted to do better. After experiencing a hip-hop dance event, he was hooked. One slight problem: He didn't know how to dance. So he started to learn and practice, practice, practice. Day and night, night and day, no matter what corner of the college campus he was on, he was dancing. For two years he danced and danced and danced, perfecting his craft. There was a tryout for a rap tour with T-Pain. Adrian made it and was selected to go on tour as a back-up dancer. Traveling the country, dancing, and monetizing his passion was electrifying. Adrian was sitting with T-Pain one day. He released a song on social media, and within about 15 minutes, it had over one million downloads. Adrian was hooked. T-Pain was actually a highly successful entrepreneur and talked to Adrian about having multiple income streams and ways to make money. He was an investor, actor, and entertainer.

Adrian eventually left the tour, finished college, and started building a following with content based on YouTube related to dance. But that wasn't paying the bills, and his follower base had plateaued. So like any post-graduate person not paying the bills, he had to get a job. After working in a call center cubicle for an insurance company, Adrian knew he had to get out and he had to get out fast. He found mentors who helped him build his niche in the digital online space, build online digital products, and create his own courses on dance that people could buy right off the internet. His first promotion landed him $1,000. Not a sum of money to retire on, but proof this could work if he could scale it bigger.

Adrian took to his fans and kept asking them what they wanted. Then he built it. Adrian gave them what they wanted and did it in an authentic and valuable way. He gave himself away to those people, ensuring they were successful in accomplishing their goals, which ensured that he accomplished his.

Adrian branched out and started learning more about internet marketing, internet-based commerce, and how trends and business were forming online. Just like his dance, Adrian had no education or experience in this, but he practiced day and night, night and day, and he figured it out. Adrian has turned this passion for dance and digital business into a seven-figure annual income in just seven years. He now employs a team of more than a dozen people. Adrian now has savings income, real estate income, business income, subscription income, affiliate income, and intellectual property income from the courses he offers. Adrian is also using the money from all of that to drive investment income from the market and invest it in other businesses.

Adrian is the perfect example of when persistence meets passion. Generating multiple sources of income is possible. You just can't let anything stand in your way.

Uncommon Wealth Tactics:

Okay, we know this was a lot of information, and we want to reiterate that leveraging multiple income sources or building one or even two of these streams of income is going to take time to perfect. We want you to know the endgame and how to calculate it because we want things to be simpler to understand financially. Do you want to know approximately how much money you will need when you are financially free? Here is how to calculate this with the 4% rule.

If you have been following along with the Uncommon Financial Dashboard, you should already know your **Projected Monthly Income at Financial Freedom Date**.

Our example earlier in the book was **$10,766.95**.

Take your Projected Monthly Income at your Financial Freedom Date and divide it by 100. So in our example, 10,766.95 / 100 = 107.6695

Take that number and multiply it by 30,000. That is the number you need to generate your monthly expense. 107.6695 x 30,000 = $3,230,085

Before you shut down over the size of that number, understand that you don't need to have all of that money in one account. You could have it in one account, but a lot of our clients have a lot of things that are being added up to give them the Net Worth of $3,230,085. For starters, in this example, this could include their paid-off mortgage worth $530,000, a business valued at $870,000, a rental property that is paid off and is worth $200,000, a whole life policy with a cash value of $200,000, a 401(k) at $1,300,000, and $130,000 in the bank. All that makes up the $3,230,000 number.

And remember, you have 15 years to be able to work on all of these. These are numbers that are attainable.

What is your current Net Worth? Whatever it may be, it's a

starting point, and a way to track your progress moving forward.

Here is how you know. Take your assets and subtract your liabilities. That is your current Net Worth.

From our earlier examples in Chapters 5 and 6, let's use $1,200,000 for Assets and $634,000 in Liabilities.

Assets – Liabilities = Net Worth

1,200,000 – 634,000 = 566,000 is your Net Worth

This will now give you a chart you can use to hold yourself accountable each year, and it should look something like this:

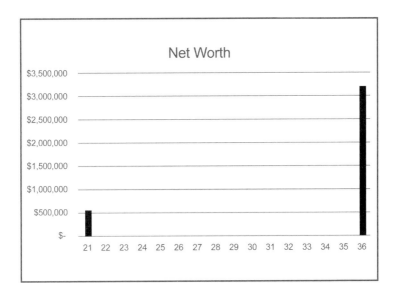

Each year, you should be able to see your net worth growing because the things you are doing are making your assets grow and your liabilities shrink.

This graph is created for you by inputting your values into our

Uncommon Financial Dashboard website. We want you to see how easy it is to break down this goal, invest in your ideas, and build wealth that helps you toward financial freedom.

CHAPTER 11

Time Freedom

What if you could spend your days exactly the way you wanted to? What if your daily schedule was not dictated by the need to earn enough money to meet your obligations? What if you were able to live life on your terms instead of just making a living?

That's what time freedom allows.

We define time freedom this way: when the monthly cash flow you are receiving from residual income sources covers your monthly expenses. Time freedom is when you can choose what to do with your time because your financial needs are covered. Time freedom means reaching the point where your monthly expenses are covered by your residual income—because financial freedom equals time freedom.

Let's just say up front that time freedom does not necessarily mean you stop working. When you have set up the previous steps the right way—your budget, your capital fund, your banking system, and your residual income and investments—you will see that not only is this sense of freedom life-giving, but it will also make you want to "retire" in a different way than other people envision.

Time Freedom Means Purpose Freedom

The best example we can give of this is Warren Buffett. Whatever you think of him, one thing is a fact: he keeps working at what he loves. He enjoys buying businesses and making them more efficient. We don't think he is doing it for the money. Money might be an indicator of how well he is doing when he buys a new business, but at this point, it is not the primary motivation. Not even close. This should remind you of our earlier example of the third bricklayer. If you are passionate about what you do and why you are doing it, why would you want to stop?

So if you do set out on this Uncommon Path the right way, it won't necessarily lead to a life of pure leisure. If you want to take a month or several months to travel the world, you could do that. But the passionate spark that drove you through the other phases of the Uncommon Path doesn't just go away when your bills get covered each month. The way you spend your time might look different when you reach time freedom and as you grow older, but you would never completely leave something that you enjoy doing. It goes back to that question we ask our clients: "If you love what you do, when do you want to stop doing it?" Probably never.

The time freedom phase is also where you can have the most impact on others. This is a time when you can guide others down their version of the Uncommon Path. Reaching time freedom means you have become something of a mentor. People listen to results. Of course, you will have a significant impact on other people in other phases of the Uncommon Path, but when you get to the Time Freedom Phase, you have the success that people are drawn to.

Time freedom is the goal to shoot for when you first start the Uncommon Path.

100%

If you have not started down the Uncommon Path, the idea of time freedom probably sounds daunting. You may be facing down an income shortfall or a lot of debt you have obtained. Time freedom means going from potentially 0% residual income to time freedom (what others would call retirement) where you receive 100% residual income.

When you first start out, this chasm seems like a huge obstacle.

For most people, the typical retirement looks like this: work for years, wait until you are 59-and-a-half or older, then begin doing what you've always dreamed of doing. Alternatively, time freedom is when your passion and your career are intertwined, where you can't wait to get up in the morning because you know that the day ahead of you is filled with exactly what you choose to do.

Where are you right now? Typical retirement has a defined time frame around it, whereas time freedom does not. We have clients who are 26 years old and are already in the time freedom mindset. They are loving life because they were willing to think uncommonly.

Here's an email response we received recently from a young client:

> *Hey!*
>
> *I've taken a spontaneous trip to see the world's tallest building in person, and some man-made islands shaped like palm trees. Can you guess where I am?*

You might be thinking that he is young and probably doesn't have a family and kids to worry about, and you would be right. But we see in his mindset that he will likely always pursue his passions, no matter his life circumstances. He is locked into a way of living where he has a time freedom mindset. Once you have that, you don't go back to thinking about traditional retirement.

Another individual we have met with loves airplanes. After some encouragement, he is not only pursuing his pilot's license, he's also pursuing buying an airport that would pay him to do what he loves! Challenge yourself to think uncommonly and start having a time freedom mindset before you retire.

Don't get us wrong, there is nothing wrong with going the traditional retirement route, and we have many clients doing just that and enjoying what they do every day. We are excited for each of them to walk out of their workplace for the last time before retirement. I am sure it will feel like the last day of school before summer.

Do you love what you do? Do you enjoy going to work in the morning? If you don't, we would challenge you to start thinking of things you can do that will get you to where you want to go. Don't hate your job for 43 years only to retire and hope that your next 20 years will be better. Start living your life now! We are not guaranteed tomorrow. What are you passionate about? What age do you really want time freedom? Is it going to take a different mindset to get there? If you adopted this new mindset, could you get there sooner than you thought? Time is a precious commodity, so enjoy what you do and how you do it. It just might take some Uncommon Thinking to get there.

Systematizing Time Freedom

Since we are saying that you will still be operating within your passion and generating income from several sources, how do you systematize your income to keep getting more efficient? How do we set up your income so it is not contingent on you being there?

Automating investment accounts to pay you is simple once you have the balance built up to sustain the income you are taking. But beyond that, how do you automate a real estate portfolio, a business, or your royalty income to work for you as well?

Step 1 – Residual income meets monthly expenses, but we cannot take our hands off the wheel.

Step 2 – The system is automated and can run when someone takes a month off.

Step 3 – You could sell the system or hire into the system, and the portion you can take out more than exceeds your needs. You may be burnt out or have an idea to start something completely different.

Step 4 – Creating a system where you can mentor other people to build success in a similar way you did, giving back, and creating exponential wealth with a team of people.

What Would You Do with Time Freedom?

Everyone has a different definition of success. Everyone has a different number they need to cover their monthly "nut." It's the same with time freedom. What have your dreams and expectations been for a standard 65-plus retirement scenario? What would it take to make that happen sooner rather than later? The Uncommon Path starts with questions like that.

So you've reached that point where your monthly expenses are covered by your residual income investments. What does that look like?

Some will hop on a cruise ship and travel around the world. Some might join a global build for Habitat for Humanity. Some might stay right where they are and not alter their routine one iota.

The beauty of time freedom is that it is yours to do as you please.

Protecting Your Legacy

At this point of the book and this point in your life, there is one certainty. Things will not go as you plan them. That is a part of life. In the age of social media, comparison can be the thief of joy. Everyone in life goes through hardships, setbacks, and unexpected events. So protecting your legacy takes planning, and it is often neglected. Your biggest risks in life as you age are:

1. **Health**
2. **Disability**
3. **Death**
4. **Assisted Living / Nursing Homes / Critical Illness**

Healthcare

Having a plan for health insurance or health-related expenses is critical to a solid financial plan. It is the first type of insurance you should purchase and is now largely mandated under current legislation. If you are younger than 65, you are not eligible for Medicare, but you have several options to choose from. Our clients on Medicare love it. We haven't heard anyone complain about it yet. Even so, medical expenses can be a lot in retirement as you age. Not so much on the things covered by Medicare, but on those that aren't. Specifically, dental, vision, and hearing, which are not covered under Medicare.

Most find a supplemental insurance they like, and once it is set up, it's simple. The other expenses are where you can really get caught flat-footed. A new set of teeth put in your mouth, new hearing aids, and a pair of glasses could set you back $30,000 in one year.

Some folks get a gym membership as part of their Medicare supplement coverage. So there are things you need to look for that are meaningful to you. This is why we advocate for maintaining a corporate structure, even in retirement—if you can keep it with a health reimbursement account (HRA)—because it allows you to deduct your Medicare supplement expense, your dental, vision, and hearing expenses, and any preventative or proactive medical treatments that you may be getting as it relates to the approved expenses under the IRS code. Consulting businesses, property management, or financing companies are great business ideas to maintain a corporate structure and income.

If you have a medical situation that impacts your ability to work beyond 90 days, then you would be legally termed disabled. Let's look at that risk next.

Disability Insurance

Disability insurance is probably our least-sold type of insurance because nobody wants to buy it, and nobody thinks it will happen to them. Protecting your future income-earning potential, though, is critical. Many of our clients are covered through quality plans through their employer. That being said, leaving one employer and joining another may result in the loss of that employee benefit. So owning it personally is recommended if you see yourself venturing out or changing careers.

Let's say you are 40 years old. Your largest income-earning years are most likely still ahead of you unless you are an entertainer or professional athlete. The average American typically earns their highest wages between 50 and 65. So protecting that future income and ability to build wealth is very important.

Purchasing disability insurance protects you against the loss of income and can be tailored in multiple ways to your personal situation. It covers retirement contributions and residual disability if you are able to go back to work but not earn as much as you were making before the disability.

The other important thing, especially as an entrepreneur, is layering coverages so insurance works together. In the event you are disabled, the insurance company no longer makes you pay your premium on your disability insurance. Now, let's look at how you can combine that with your life insurance coverage to protect you further since death is also an obvious risk.

Life Insurance

As you could gather from Chapter 7 and Uncommon Banking, we structure life insurance as an asset and a positive cash flow source because it is critical to have a plan that generates income on savings. With that, we do pick up a death benefit that compounds or grows over time as your net worth and wealth grow. This helps you in retirement or the latter stages of your life since it can provide your estate or loved ones with critical tax-free liquidity to help with your loss. For the families that Uncommon Banking doesn't make sense for, we do recommend term life insurance.

Looking at a death benefit from the perspective of true income protection and looking at the fact that your highest income-earning years are from 50 to 65, the younger you are, typically the more the insurance company will underwrite you for. Life insurance is underwritten or evaluated by the insurance company based off of income or net worth. When you are 25 to 40, the insurance companies will typically underwrite you for 30 times your annual salary.

Forty-one to 55 is normally 20 times your annual salary since your income should have gone up and you are 10 years older. From 56 to 70, insurance companies are looking at insuring to around 10 times your income since you are now much older and have fewer income-earning years ahead. Also, as you age and build wealth, your overall investments and net worth should have grown as well, so you would be leaving behind other assets in addition to a death benefit.

If you are looking for true income replacement, and if we looked at the 4% rule we talked about in Chapter 2, we advocate for never being below 20 times your annual income, especially if you still have a mortgage payment and young children. Let's look at a 35-year-old male making $100,000 gross a year. At only 20 times his annual gross salary, that gives us $2,000,000 in death benefit. Now subtract, let's say, $150,000 for a mortgage, funeral expense of say $15,000, and a car balance of $15,000. After that, there is $1,820,000 left over. After other expenses, other bills, and maybe picking up some things to make life easier, let's just call it $1,800,000. At 4%, that is only $72,000 a year of income if you didn't want to spend down principal and run the risk of running out of money. This is a much truer income-replacement scenario and how you protect your young family in the event of your premature departure.

We think it helps to frame it by looking at life insurance from the death benefit standpoint and checking to see where your coverages are relative to your needs and goals.

Assisted Living/Nursing Home/Critical Illness

Let's face it, this is one thing no one is looking forward to. If you have had a loved one in a nursing home, it can be a point of great sadness and loss. Planning for the end of your life can be difficult, but planning it now is critical if you want it to happen on your terms, especially financially.

Long-term care insurance has been around for a long time. However, it has changed a lot over the last several years as many insurance carriers mispriced their insurance offerings and have had to raise prices or reduce benefits to keep up with the costs and claims they are paying out.

Many don't want to buy long-term care insurance because it's expensive, and they feel like if they don't use it, it's a ton of money out the window.

We look at it more holistically since most people want three things as they age. They want to be paid interest on their cash like they used to. They naturally want more cash as they age. Their risk level and attention change. They typically want a death benefit or the peace of mind of knowing they will leave some sort of financial benefit behind to loved ones or charity. Lastly, they want to be taken care of with dignity in their last stages of life.

We feel like we can accomplish those three things with one solution: Life insurance—boring, old, whole life insurance. See, the insurance companies weren't so great at pricing the risk of longevity and long-term care expense, but they are great at pricing the mortality risk, which they have been doing successfully for hundreds of years. The insurance companies know on a whole life policy what their risk is. They know that the client is going to get the benefit one way or another, so to provide the client with a way to access the death benefit for critical illness care is in their best interest and for the good of the marketplace. So we typically design and solve for these things with a policy designed to accrue cash value. This way, you have access to your savings with a guaranteed rate of return and a cost structure that can't go up. You also have a guaranteed death benefit that can be used as life insurance or to help fund a critical expense like assisted living, home healthcare, or a nursing home.

It is critical to prepare the legal documents now to make sure your wishes are known. This protects your legacy and helps your loved ones deal with your loss more easily. We have all heard horror stories of how that one person passed away, and their family took years figuring out where everything was and settling the estate. Let's look at the basic documents you need to protect your legacy.

Wills and Trusts

Your last will and testament is a document most of us are familiar with. Having that document finalized is helpful to closing your estate. If you have more assets or want more control from the grave (as they call it) to protect family or whatever the reason may be, you can set up a trust.

A last will and testament usually points to a trust, then a trust document is created, which provides more ability to dictate and control your assets and legacy. The trust document can be its own entity and act after you pass, depending on the language within.

Within your will and testament, you will list an Executor, the person appointed to handle or be the leader of finalizing your estate in the event of your death. That person is only appointed upon your death, not before.

These documents typically govern who will receive your possessions that aren't listed at an investment firm, like your home, cars, collectibles, and heirlooms.

Let's examine more of the documents used to help protect you if your health or mental abilities decline, but you are still living.

Living Will

What happens if you are incapacitated, in a coma, or in some other situation like that? A Living Will is a living health directive that lists whether you want to be resuscitated or have your organs donated, and who can make health-related decisions on your behalf if you aren't conscious while receiving medical attention. This person only has the authority to make health-related decisions, not financial.

Power of Attorney

As with a living will, a Power of Attorney gives someone else legal authority to act on your behalf for financial, investment, and business-related matters. You are still alive but are not in the right mental or cognitive state to make decisions in your best interest or the interest of others. The Power of Attorney is separate from the living will and does not govern health-related decisions unless it's specifically a healthcare power of attorney.

Beneficiary Designations

What happens to your accounts is important, and the way you title your assets and accounts is important. We touched on this a bit in Chapter 6, where we had you list out your assets. The way your assets are registered is important because each registration carriers its own tax laws and tax consequences. Beneficiaries listed on retirement accounts like 401(k), 403(b), 457, pensions, IRAs, and Roth IRAs supersede your Will and Trust directives. If the beneficiary is designated differently on those accounts from your will and/or trust, then the company that has those accounts will follow the beneficiary designation that was used to open the account. So this is important to review annually or when you have a change in your estate plans.

You can also list beneficiaries on after-tax designations like an Individual Account or Joint With Rights of Survivorship account by adding a Transfer on Death (TOD) designation to the account. This lists the beneficiaries and helps that asset transition to the listed party and move outside of probate after you "graduate."

Ensure with your attorney and financial advisor that your beneficiary designations and accounts are titled and registered as you wish and that your legal documents listed above all match so that your wishes are carried out if something happens to you.

Time to Build Your Legacy

Dreams may start with what you as an individual are passionate about, but they always, always wind up with a desire to reach beyond yourself.

We all want to leave a legacy.

An important aspect of time freedom, now that your lifestyle is covered, is that you can also think about the legacy you want to leave—for your children and grandchildren or other loved ones. We were introduced to a book a while back from another advisor, and after reading it, we were hooked. The book is called *The Brower Quadrant* by Lee Brower. Brower lays out the four main aspects of legacy in his book. We thought it was so good that it has informed the way we think and speak about the topic of legacy.

The four quadrants are Core Values (who you are), Experience Assets (what you've done), Contribution Assets (what you've given back to your community), and Financial Assets (what you will leave behind). The premise and purpose of the book is to stop focusing on your money as your legacy and start focusing on the other three quadrants. Brower's main takeaway in the book is that if you could only leave three of the quadrants behind as your legacy, which three would you choose?

Like you, we always choose Core Assets, Experience Assets, and Contribution Assets—not money. If you invest your money now into those three, your children and grandchildren will not need your money. Brower also then helps families communicate all of this to their loved ones and create an environment to have a family conversation.

A Glimpse Down the Uncommon Path:

A Family Conversation – James and Gwenn Ehlers

There are lots of ways to share your legacy, your values and beliefs, your good and bad experiences, your contributions and charity, as well as your financial resources. A few years ago, we also started helping our clients through their very own Family Conversations.

Here is the history behind our first Family Conversation. We were working with Jim and Gwenn for months on their estate and retirement plan. We collaborated with their attorney and CPA to make sure we presented a very thought-out plan that covered every one of their desires and answered every objection they had at the beginning of the process. It was a neat plan.

As we closed the final meeting, they thanked us, and then in passing, one of them said, "How do we tell our kids what we just put in place?" When they both turned to look at us, we knew there had to be more to this process. That's when we started offering the Family Conversation. We realized that just doing an estate plan is only half the battle. The real power is when you can have someone help lead the whole family through the entire plan and allow the children or the next generation to ask questions.

We took a full two days with the whole family. We met with Jim and Gwenn, their three children, and the spouses of the two married children. The first day, we focused on the values that the family held in high regard, what shaped them into the people they are today, and lastly, what things the younger generation had learned from their parents throughout the years. We were all laughing hysterically one minute and crying the next. It was one of the neatest things we have ever been a part of, to see this family who has had so many years together be able to laugh together as well as process deeper issues. It was such a healing time for everyone! That was the first day.

The second day was more of the nuts and bolts of what we had put in place. We allowed the parents to communicate what they wanted to achieve by doing the estate plan, then we helped articulate some of the more detailed points of the plan. At the end, we allowed each person to ask questions or clarify in more detail any part of the plan. After the meeting was done, one of the children said how much they respected and loved their parents for having the hard conversation and allowing them into the details of their plan.

To this day, we have a great relationship with everyone in the family, and we plan to have a lasting relationship with each one of them because we were able to facilitate a family conversation about a hard topic.

So when you begin to shape your legacy, we encourage you to find a way to have an open and frank conversation with everyone your plans will impact.

Uncommon Wealth Tactics:

We laid out earlier in the chapter some basic information about protecting your wealth and legacy. This section of the dashboard is merely a checklist to quickly determine gaps in your risk management strategy. If you have one of these things in place and can confidently point to it or find it, then check the box off. If you don't have one of these things completed or are not sure, then leave it unchecked and move that item to your one-year goal section of the form.

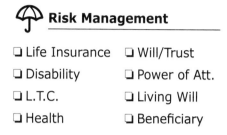

Risk Management

- ❏ Life Insurance
- ❏ Disability
- ❏ L.T.C.
- ❏ Health
- ❏ Will/Trust
- ❏ Power of Att.
- ❏ Living Will
- ❏ Beneficiary

Putting It All Together

Now that you have finished the book it is time to compile your Uncommon Financial Dashboard. This is what it will look like:

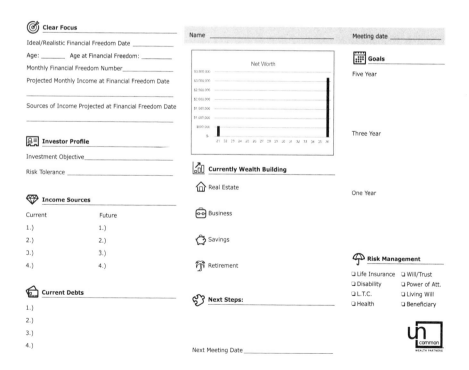

You Did It!

When you get to that point of time freedom, there is nothing like it. It's an amazing feeling.

We are not here to sell you sunshine and unicorns. The Uncommon Path is not easy, and it's not a get-rich-quick plan. But it is an approach we have seen bear fruit time and time again. And since it is built on how God has uniquely gifted you, no two paths are the same. That's what makes our work so exciting—we get to help people discover and map out their own unique path!

When you get real about your numbers with a budget and invest in yourself and build residual sources of income, you can achieve time freedom.

Does this mean a life of complete leisure? For some, it might. But most of the time, when people love what they do—the thing that gives them energy and purpose—they are happy to just keep doing that in some form or another.

Time freedom does mean you can set your own schedule, your business concerns can function without you there day-to-day, and you know your bases are covered now and into the future.

The path to get there is up to you, but know that this is possible. When you set out on the Uncommon Path, that end goal of time freedom is possible, maybe sooner than you think!

The time is now. As we outlined in Chapter 1, Central Banks around the world are racing to 0% interest rates to stimulate economies, and our world is awash in debt. Money is getting cheaper, and you have more dollars chasing fewer goods. With automation and robots coming at an alarming pace, there has never been a better time to be true to yourself and carve out your niche in this world.

The internet and social media help us find those people who are like us, who value what we value, and connect us. The opportunity to share information and education is better than ever. Everything is being deinstitutionalized, and that is a good thing for entrepreneurship. In a world that is so connected through social media, many are reporting that most Americans feel lonelier than ever. Depression and mental illness are at an all-time high. When we pursue our gifts, our calling, and our vocation, we are energized. We feel alive and purposeful. We share that energy and purpose with the world, and we touch people's lives. When we see those videos where someone is using their gifts to touch another life, it is pure, raw, and emotional. Cats chasing laser pointers and Grandpa-falling-down videos just don't compare.

The world is starving for what is within you. That thing inside of you that makes you unique—dare we say uncommon. We are asking you to embrace it, document it, and share it with the world. Those who do never regret it, and what they learn about themselves is worth more than money. That mindset is contagious, and we are here to say you can do it. You must do it. Time is of the essence. The world needs the Uncommon within you!

Go forth and be Uncommon!

The
Uncommon
Life Project

Don't miss a single episode!

Every episode of The Uncommon Life Project explores how someone got very intentional about the life they wanted to lead and what it would take to get there. Hear their dreams, stories, challenges, and ultimately, triumphs!

www.uncommonwealth.com/podcast